Nap

120th
anniversary

Berlitz

- A ☛ in the text denotes a highly recommended sight
- A complete A–Z of practical information starts on p.105
- Extensive mapping on cover flaps

Berlitz Publishing Company, Inc.

Princeton   Mexico City   Dublin   Eschborn   Singapore

Text: Don Allan
Editors: Jane Middleton
Photography: Claude Huber
Layout: Media Content Marketing, Inc.
Cartography: GeoSystems

Found an error we should know about? Our editor would be happy to hear from you, and a postcard would do. Although we make every effort to ensure the accuracy of all the information in this book, changes do occur.

ISBN 2-8315-6418-2
Revised 1998 – First Printing April 1998

Printed in Switzerland by Weber SA, Bienne
019/804 REV

CONTENTS

NAPLES

THE REGION AND ITS PEOPLE

Naples is a theatre. Its buildings are ranged on hillsides like box seats encircling a stage. And what a set! Viewed from the heights, a castle seems to plunge like a ship into the waves of a blue sea, there's a sail or two on the water, the coastline curls past the purple cone of Vesuvius towards Sorrento's cape, and Capri floats in a distant haze. Add a little mandolin music and you've got the curtain going up on Act I.

On the corner, a crone knits beside a tray of contraband cigarettes she's selling, ignored by two policemen. They are arguing about football. From a doorway, where two men are playing cards, an appetizing smell of cooking drifts into the street. Near a church, someone consults a guidebook—that's *you*, the tourist, a part of the action, too.

From dramatic Naples it is just a short ferry ride to Capri, Ischia, and the Amalfi coast. Nowadays most vacationers hurry straight to the docks and glimpse the city only in transit to these siren lands, or on a day's excursion to Pompeii and Vesuvius. A new generation of travellers has forgotten that Naples is one of Europe's oldest and greatest cities, the capital of an ancient kingdom and the goal of all would-be sophisticates making the Continental "Grand Tour." The vitality behind the poverty, and the beauty amid squalor, have always been part and parcel of the contradictions of Naples. It may come as a surprise to find that its treasures are all still here.

Campania, the region Naples rules, is justly praised as spectacularly beautiful. It used to be the Roman Riviera, devoted to a pleasure and luxury still beckoning in the ruins of

Pompeii and Herculaneum, and never more seductive than today in the *dolce far niente* of jet-set "fishing villages" and flowery café terraces high above the sparkling sea. The Ravello that captivated Wagner in the 19th century wooed Garbo with the same charms in the 20th. The Sorrento that Caruso loved still echoes his serenade.

Campania is famous too, as the birthplace of that world citizen, the pizza; as the unchallenged champion of pasta cookery, with sauces based on plump tomatoes grown in the rich volcanic soil surrounding Vesuvius; and as the home of irresistible ice-creams, an Italian gift to humanity. The fires that smoulder beneath Vesuvius heat the waters and radioactive mud of Campanian mineral spas, renowned for their healing properties for 2,000 years. So if you overindulge in the wonderful food of the region, a cure is at hand.

Much of Campania is volcanic. Arriving by air, you look down on a landscape scarred with the escarpments and basins of old craters. It still leaks steam at the seams and is shaken from time to time by tremors, including one in 1980 that killed more than 2,000 people in the province. Vesuvius preserved for posterity the time-warp museum cities of Pompeii and Herculaneum by burying

The rugged beauty of the Amalfi coast meets the sea.

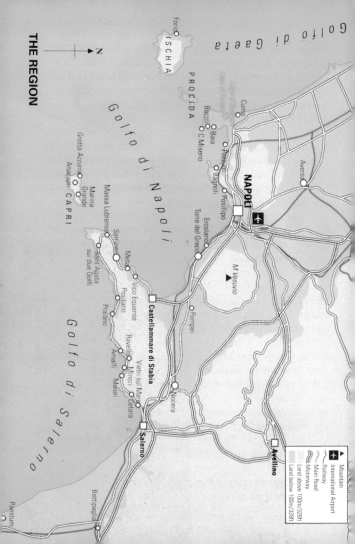

them in 79 A.D. It last erupted in 1944, and hasn't finished yet. The people can be volcanic, too. A group on a street corner whose voices and gestures seem to verge on mayhem may just be having a friendly chat. Neapolitan hand and body language can communicate hundreds of messages without words, and words without gestures in southern Italy would be like pasta without the sauce.

The Neapolitan shrug, meaning anything from "Who knows?" to "What do you expect me to do about it?," is the world's greatest shrug. The local dialect can be incomprehensible to Italians from the North. Word endings tend to drop off and diminutives are added to everything.

Having served (and out-witted) many foreign rulers, the working people of the region have evolved a practice of flattery that is totally tongue-in-cheek. Almost any reasonably well-dressed male adult will be called "*Dottore*" (i.e. a person with a university degree, not a doctor of medicine). A little grey hair will earn the title "*Professore*." Locally, a man of power and/or dignity may be addressed as "*Don*," a tradition from the Spanish era. Unfortunately, none of

A balcony in the Neapolitan Riviera graced with colourful fruits and greenery.

9

this implies genuine respect, for such is not in the cynical Neapolitan's nature.

The southerner's loyalty is to the family. On holidays, restaurants will be full of three- and four-generation family gatherings. At picnic spots a friendly stranger will often be invited to share. On Sundays young couples with children will be seen carrying neatly packaged pastries and bunches of flowers, on their way to visit *La Nonna*—Grandma. Graves are regularly tended and decorated with flowers, as are street shrines that are often dedicated to a departed parent. Many a family is supported by the remittances of a member working abroad.

Unemployment in the Mezzogiorno, as the South is known, is almost twice the national average. Naples itself is haunted by a violent history and tattered trappings of bygone glory. These days, when the city is most notorious for poverty, crime, congestion, and inefficient services, when its sons and daughters leave home to find work in the North and abroad, the proud claim *Vide Napoli e poi morí*—

The magnificent Amalfi coast is a favourite get-away for locals and tourists.

"See Naples and die"—has a sardonic rather than a boastful ring.

These are things to consider before accepting the stereotype of what the people of the Bay of Naples are supposed to be. Consider, too, the amazing history that has flowed and settled over Naples and its environs. Instead of a freeze-frame of a moment in the past, as captured in Pompeii, this is a living, brawling family, proud of its genealogy and its heirlooms, still growing, hospitable, but struggling to make ends meet.

A BRIEF HISTORY

The Greeks and Romans

Naples was founded in the seventh century B.C., probably by Greeks already established in Cuma or Ischia who called it Neapolis, the "New City," to distinguish it from the older nearby settlement of Parthenope. (According to legend, Parthenope was one of the sirens who tried to lure Ulysses ashore by their songs. Failing, she threw herself into the sea, and the colony supposedly guarded her grave.) Only a few traces of ancient wall remain of the Greek city. Naples has been repeatedly rebuilt on the same site, incorporating bits of the old as construction materials.

The city states of Magna Grecia, as the coast of southern Italy was known, squabbled among themselves for centuries, never achieving strength in unity. This made them easy prey to the well-organized Romans, and Naples became a vassal of Rome in 328 B.C. The city clung to its Greek heritage and language, however, and it became a centre of culture for Roman parvenus. They sent their sons here to gain polish, and they built amphitheatres, sumptuous baths, and luxurious vacation villas on the shores of the lovely bay.

Byzantine Emperors, Norman Barons, and Angevin Kings

Following the collapse of the Roman Empire and the ensuing disintegration of Roman and Greek civilization, barbarians from the north captured most of the Neapolitan hinterland, and Naples turned to the Byzantine emperors of Constantinople for support. Greek again became the official language of the city, which was then ruled by a series of dukes. When one of these submitted to the authority of the Pope in Rome in A.D. 763, the links with Byzantium were broken, and for nearly 400 years an independent Duchy of Naples held off would-be invaders, including a new force that swept out of the Middle East and captured Sicily— the Muslim Saracens. The era of independence was doomed, however, by the arrival in southern Italy of the Normans, who conquered Sicily and most of the territory that later became the Kingdom of Naples and Sicily. Norman architecture in many of the castles and churches throughout the South is one lasting legacy of their power.

In 1266, after a century of struggles and intrigue between various dynasties,

Treasures from Charles III's Capodimonte Palace, which is now a museum.

and a period of rule by the German Hohenstaufens, the Pope declared the young brother of King Louis IX of France, Charles of Anjou, to be the rightful sovereign of Sicily and Naples. The Angevins maintained control one way or another until 1435, but this period was punctuated by Sicilian rebellion and a protracted, desultory war with the Aragons of Spain.

Spanish Rule

In 1343, 17-year-old Giovanna I ascended the throne. After murdering her first husband, she married three more times and was herself assassinated in 1381. The plot thickened hopelessly, with two rival popes backing contenders from France and Hungary, numerous murders, and, finally, the adoption of an heir by Queen Giovanna II, who had many lovers but no children. The adopted heir, Alfonso V of Aragon, thus also became Alfonso I of Naples in 1442, beginning an era of Spanish domination that lasted for the next three centuries.

Casa del Fauna in Pompeii –
a glimpse back to
everyday Roman life.

During the late 15th and early 16th centuries the Italian peninsula was in constant turmoil, first through bloody rivalry between France and Spain, and then in the battles to repulse Turkish invasions. Naples was a pawn in these struggles. Spanish rule gained a strong foothold in 1504, when King Ferdinand of Spain (the sponsor of Columbus) made his military chief, Gonzalo de Cordoba, "El Gran Capitan," viceroy in Naples. There followed some 60 viceroys until 1734. Pedro de Toledo, viceroy from 1532–1553, cleaned up the city, installing sewers, pushing back the walls, and carving out the central boulevard that bears his name today.

Perhaps because of Spanish clericalism, the humanizing spirit of the Renaissance was slow to reach Naples; at the same time, though, the tolerant Neapolitans prevented the Spanish Inquisition from taking hold. Spain's artistic influence is seen in the Baroque architecture of churches and palaces, including the Palazzo Reale and a (then) new university that now houses the National Museum.

The viceroys ruled as absolute monarchs and exacted heavy taxes on all that came and went through the city gates. In 1647, discontented Neapolitan liberals engineered an uprising, ostensibly led by a fisherman named Tommaso Aniello (known as Masaniello), who proclaimed the Parthenopean Republic, with himself a *generalissimo*. This was going too far for his backers. Masaniello was assassinated and the revolt was quashed the following year. The unhappy city was then hit by a plague in 1656 that carried off 400,000 people in six months.

All Europe became embroiled in the War of the Spanish Succession (1701–1714) to decide whether French Bourbon or Austrian Habsburg claimants should take the vacant throne in Spain. Philip V, a Bourbon, was crowned in

Madrid, but in the treaties ending the war Naples passed to Habsburg Austria. Austrian-appointed viceroys governed Naples until 1734, when Philip's son Charles chased them out and entered Naples to wild rejoicing as Charles III, first of the Bourbon kings of Naples and Sicily, a realm comprising the lower half of the Italian boot, from Gaeta to Pescara, Sicily, Sardinia, and the smaller islands.

Charles brought with him one of Europe's finest collections of art and antiquities, and added to it by supporting the first excavations of Pompeii and other sites. Charles also inherited the Bourbon urge to build palaces: Caserta and Capodimonte, as well as the San Carlo opera house, were among his many embellishments of the kingdom. His Naples was a brilliant capital, a thriving port and one of the largest cities of Europe.

Revolution and Unification

By the time of the French Revolution, Charles's son Ferdinando I and IV (so-called because he was I of the Two Sicilies and IV of Naples) was on the throne. This extremely uncouth monarch—his greatest joys were hunting and fishing in company with the lowest of his subjects, who called him "Nasone" because of his very long nose—was married to a sister of Marie Antoinette, and so Naples allied with England, Austria, and Russia against Republican France. When French armies approached his capital, the king and his numerous brood were smuggled aboard a British warship commanded by Admiral Horatio Nelson and taken to safety in Sicily. The upper-class intellectuals then opened the gates of Naples to the French and proclaimed a second Parthenopean Republic; the *lazzeroni* (the lower classes) fought for their king. The second republic lasted only a few months, and although promised an amnesty if they surrendered, the leaders were actually executed in the Piazza del Mercato. Nelson himself commanded that the Republican Admiral Caracciolo be hanged from a yard arm and then thrown overboard. (This was at the same time as Nelson's celebrated affair with Lady Emma Hamilton, who was the wife of the British Ambassador to Naples.)

Ferdinando IV had to flee to Sicily a second time in 1806, when Napoleon sent an army to put his brother Joseph on the throne of Naples. Two years later Napoleon promoted Joseph to be King of Spain and replaced him in

A scuplture of knights at the Castel Nuovo in Naples.

Naples with his brother-in-law, Joachim Murat. The English fleet took Capri briefly and bombarded Ischia. After the fall of Napoleon and Murat, Ferdinando was restored to power, this time as Ferdinando I of the Kingdom of the Two Sicilies. In 1820 a mutiny in the army under General Guillermo Pepe forced the king to grant a constitution, but it was abolished when Austrian troops came to Ferdinando's aid and restored the status quo. Three more Bourbon kings—Francesco I, Ferdinando II, and Francesco II—followed, all noted for their misrule and their complete disregard of the changes sweeping Europe. In 1848 Ferdinando II responded to agitation for more democracy by creating a constitutional parliament and then throwing its leading members in jail. These events prompted the British Prime Minister Gladstone's famous condemnation of the Bourbon regime as "the negation of God erected into a system of government."

When Giuseppe Garibaldi debarked in Sicily in May 1860 with his One Thousand, fighters for Italian unification, he had little difficulty defeating the Bourbon troops and swelling his own small army as it rapidly advanced toward Naples. In desperation, Francesco II, king for barely a year, granted a constitution, then, in September, fled as the city turned out *en masse* to welcome Garibaldi. A plebiscite overwhelmingly approved the union of Naples and Sicily with the new Kingdom of Italy under King Vittorio Emanuele II of Savoy.

The Twentieth Century

This extraordinarily eventful history has left Naples and its surrounding region with a vast array of monuments to the succession of Greek, Roman, Norman, Hohenstaufen, Angevin, Aragonese, Spanish, and Bourbon dynasties, but the former kingdom of Naples and Sicily is today the poorest part of Italy. Much of the immigration of Italians to North and South America and the seasonal flood of migrant Italian field and construction workers into northern Europe has come from the lands once ruled from Naples.

Under Mussolini the South was a place of exile, an Italian Siberia. In 1943, during World War II, Allied armies landed at Salerno in 1943. Naples was bombed frequently, and the departing German army burned the ancient archives of the city. The harbour, packed with ships protected by barrage balloons, became an important supply link for the Allied forces—and a bonanza for Neapolitan smugglers and black marketeers. Caserta became the American headquarters. While Mussolini and the Germans held Rome and the North of Italy, the South joined the Allies as a "co-belligerent" under Marshall Badoglio. After the war, traditionally monarchist Naples voted against the creation of the present Republic of Italy.

In an effort to alleviate the poverty of the region the *Cassa per il Mezzogiorno*, the Fund for the South, was created in the 1950s. Factories, steel mills, and power plants were built, the *autostrada* network was extended, swampy lands were drained, and agriculture modernized. However, many of the attempts at industrialization have failed. The worldwide decline in shipping has reduced the importance of the port. The ancient criminal brotherhood, the Camorra, older than the Mafia, has revived as the Nuova Camorra Organizzata, and thrives on rackets and the drug trade. Fortunately for visitors, the violence is almost entirely confined to the invisible underworld.

Today, many see tourism as the major growth industry for Naples and its enchanting hinterland, as it was in the days of the Grand Tour.

WHERE TO GO

One of the great advantages of visiting Naples and its region is that its many very different points of interest for art, history, scenic beauty, and leisure are all within easy reach of each other. You won't have to make agonizing choices between seeing Sorrento or Pompeii or dining on a Capri terrace. You can do it all in a single day, though rushing is not to be recommended.

Naples and the Neapolitans make up a fascinating, if chaotic, urban organism that outsiders tend not to take seriously until they discover that the city is a kind of living museum. Finding its treasures is an adventure that leads from the bay to the heights, through cyclonic traffic and narrow byways where high-decibel family life spills out into the streets.

The Castel dell'Ovo is an ideal starting point for a walking tour of Naples.

Even tourists looking forward to relaxing at one of the seaside resorts or islands shouldn't miss the Naples experience.

A car can be useful outside the city, though the network of buses, trains, and boats is quite efficient. In Naples itself, a car is really a handicap and is best left in a garage. Traffic is fierce and parking virtually impossible. Buses, the metro (as the subway/underground train system, metropolitana, is known), and funiculars can take you to within walking distance of major attractions, and taxis are not expensive.

Come prepared to walk, for whether in the back streets of Old Naples, older Pompeii, or oldest Paestum, this is the way to enter into the spirit of the place. The itineraries that follow are designed to lead you to discover this spirit for yourself.

NAPLES

The Seafront

A four-lane, one-way boulevard ceaselessly humming with traffic skirts an arc of the photogenic seafront west to east, from the bustling island-ferry docks of Mergellina to the headland of Pizzofalcone above the most prominent landmark of Naples, the islet fortress **Castel dell'Ovo**. Past Pizzofalcone, a second arc takes in the city centre and shipping piers. Crossing this motorized flood is a daunting prospect. There's one crossing-place by the causeway to the Castel dell'Ovo, a good place to begin exploring Naples.

The Roman patrician Lucullus had a villa on the headland and an annex on the rocks offshore where the fortress looms. Some of the annex's columns went into the construction of a fifth-century monastery here that was transformed into a fort by the Normans in the 12th century. Thereafter the garrisons of successive dynasties came and went through its gates, as through a revolving door. A military installation until 1963, the fortress includes dungeons and barracks that have slowly been converted into halls for exhibits and conventions. In the Middle Ages a legend grew that the castle was the work of Virgil, who built it on an egg in a jar under the sea—hence the name, "Castle of the Egg."

The yacht-filled harbour in the shadow of the castle is the **Porto di Santa Lucia**—*the* Santa Lucia of the quintessential Neapolitan song that hails the city: "*O bella Napoli/ O suol beato/ Ove sorridere/ Volle il Creato*" ("O lovely Naples, blessed land, where Nature wanted to smile"). When the song was written in 1835 the Santa Lucia district under Pizzofalcone was a fish market and the home of fishermen. Now the harbour is an obligatory port of call for the hungry tourist. Seafood restaurants line the docks and the back-

Neapolitan fisherman gear up for a day of work.

streets of the Borgo Marinaro under the castle walls. Following the shoreline past Santa Lucia, the Via Partenope becomes the Via Nazario Sauro. Men like to fish here with long poles that reach out over the rocks. Ahead are the moles and cranes of the main piers of the Naples harbour, as well as the Cala Beverello landing for hydrofoils to Sorrento and the islands. Where the street rises to the left, cut across a park to the massive **Castel Nuovo**.

Many landmarks of Naples have two or more names, official and popular. The Castel Nuovo — the "New" Castle of 1279, as opposed to the old Castel dell'Ovo — is commonly called the Maschio Angioino, the Angevin Fortress, because it was built by Charles I of Anjou. However, it is really more Spanish than French. The grim, grey towers and the contrasting white Triumphal Arch were commissioned by Alfonso of Aragon in 1442, and the arch represents his defeat of the French and entry into Naples. Note the finely wrought figures under the arch and over the doorway of the Santa Barbara Chapel to the right rear of the court. Most of the apartments entered from the inner courtyard are government offices.

A section of the castle has been converted into a museum, the **Museo Civico di Castel Nuovo,** (open 9:00 A.M.–7:00 P.M., closed Sunday). A selection of 14th- and 15th-century sculptures and frescoes is on display in the Palatine Chapel, and a collection of silver and bronze artefacts from the 15th to the 20th centries in the South Wing. Note also the tablet commemorating the uprising of September 1943, when Neapolitans expelled the Germans from their town.

Behind the Castel Nuovo is the helicopter landing pad and Maritime Station. They are at the foot of the broad Piazza Municipio, a mall of fountains (waterless) and greenery (struggling) that rises to the Palazzo Municipale, the City Hall, in line with the ramparts of the Castel Sant'Elmo and the San Martino Convent high above. Turn left at the central Vittorio Emanuele II monument into the Via San Carlo and follow it for a few blocks to that shrine of opera lovers, the **Teatro di San Carlo**. This theatre, built in exactly eight months in 1737 by Charles III, is the oldest continuously performing opera house in Europe, and surely one of the most musically significant and beautiful in the world.

> Signs: *entrata*–entrance
> *uscita*–exit
> *arrivo*–arrival
> *partenza*–departure
> *fumatori/non fumatori*–smoker/nonsmoker

It doesn't look like much from the outside, but the hall inside is dazzling. The acoustics have been pronounced superb by the great composers whose works were first performed here. This may be due to empty jars packed into the walls when the theatre was rebuilt after a fire in 1816. Stendhal, who came to the re-opening, wrote, "There's nothing in all Europe that comes close to this theatre… the eye is dazzled and the spirit ravished.…"

A rehearsal at Naples' celebrated opera house, the Teatro di San Carlo.

Rossini was the artistic director from 1815–1822 and composed ten operas for the company. He skipped out after the performance of his *Zelmira*, taking the soprano with him. As she was the conductor's girlfriend, Rossini did not try to return. In came Donizetti, who remained for 16 years, delivering a new opera every year. Bellini got his start at the San Carlo.

Verdi composed three operas for the theatre and was artistic director for the 1872 season. Caruso, originally dismissed as "only a baritone," later refused to sing at San Carlo.

The San Carlo opera season runs from December to May, but there are concerts in the theatre all year round. Tickets for other theatres, sporting events, and the like may be obtained across the street in the **Galleria Umberto I** at the box office agency. The cavernous high-vaulted, glass-roofed Galleria was a showcase when it was completed in 1890. Now its tawdry tenants do not live up to the setting.

The *numero uno* spot for people-watching is just around the corner at the **Gran Caffe Gambrinus** in the Piazza Trieste e Trento. Quite apart from its excellent ices, pastries, and sandwiches, this café is worth visiting to see the Belle Epoque decoration inside. The square, incidentally, is always called Piazza San Ferdinando, after the church in one corner. If you're here on Good Friday, you can hear its choir perform the *Stabat Mater* Pergolesi composed for San Fernando.

At this point the street opens into the vast, semicir-

Locals chat under the high vaulted glass roof in the Galleria Umberto I.

cular **Piazza del Plebiscito**, where the **Palazzo Reale** (Royal Palace) faces equestrian statues of Ferdinand I and IV and his father, Charles III of Bourbon, in front of the church of San Francesco di Paola. Ferdinand built the church in 1817 as thanks for getting his kingdom back after the fall of Napoleon and departure of Murat.

There are a number of royal residences in and around Naples. Their interiors are all very similar, having been furnished and decorated *à la Versailles* in the 18th century, and then in Neo-Baroque and Empire styles in the 19th century. The Palazzo Reale was built by Spanish viceroys in the first half of the 1600s, but it takes its character from the sojourn of the Bourbon monarchs and of Joachim Murat and his wife, Napoleo 's sister Caroline Bonaparte.

The Savo g ng Umberto I installed the statues on the façade that give a c ule history of the kingdom. From left to right, they are the N rman Roger I, Frederick II of Hohenstaufen, Charles I of A jou, Alfonso I of Aragon, the Habsburg–Spanish Emperor Charles V, Charles III of Bourbon, Murat (in a pompous pose and ridiculous uniform of his own design), and Vittorio Emmanuele II of Savoy.

The palace was badly damaged by Allied bombs in 19 3 and by the occupying re . When the Italian government recovered it, the

The Palazzo Reale is one of the many royal residences in Naples.

royal apartments had to be refurbished and refurnished. They are now arranged as a museum (open 9:00 A.M.–7:30 P.M., Tuesday through Sunday, April through October; 9:30 A.M.–1:30 P.M., Tuesday through Sunday, November through March), with paintings and appropriate period furniture brought from various sources.

The **Biblioteca Nazionale** (National Library) is on the top floor of the palace; its entrance is at the rear (open 9:00 A.M.–6:30 P.M., Saturday 9:00 A.M.–1:30 P.M., closed Sunday). Among this public library's treasures are a 1485 copy of Dante's *Divine Comedy* illustrated with Botticelli engravings; illuminated medieval manuscripts; and most of the papyrus books found in Herculaneum.

To the right of the Piazza del Plebiscito the Via Chiaia skirts the hill. It's a street of elegant shops leading to the **Piazza dei Martiri**. This is the centre for elegant but pricy boutiques, art galleries, and antiques dealers, which spread into its side-streets: the Vie Santa Caterina, Cavallerizza, Alabardieri, Filangieri, and dei Mille.

A short walk towards the bay leads to the incredibly congested Piazza Vittoria (commemorating the defeat of the Turkish fleet at Lepanto in 1571) and the entrance to the mile-long **Villa Comunale**. In this leafy seafront park all Naples comes to stroll or sit on summer evenings and on Sundays. It's a great outdoor living room and garden for families cooped up in the crowded flats of Europe's most densely populated city.

The promenade on the sea side of the park following the *lungomare* corniche, the Via Caracciolo, is one of the world's most panoramic, if you can ignore the frenetic traffic. It becomes the Via Partenope near the Piazza Vittoria and continues past the Castel dell'. Parallel to it on the far side of the park is the fashionable **Riviera di Chiaia**, once popular with English visitors. Halfway down the broad avenue, where four- and six-storey 19th-century apartment houses face the park and bay, the white Neo-Classical villa of the **Museo Pignatelli** (open 9:00 A.M.–2:00 P.M., closed Monday) dominates a large garden favoured by neighbourhood children and their nursemaids. The museum offers modern art exhibits and a modest permanent collection of ceramics. A score of sporty 19th-century carriages are displayed in an annexe.

In the middle of the Villa Comunale, Europe's oldest **Aquarium** looks its age. It was founded in 1872 by the German naturalist Anton Dohrn. On view inside are denizens of the Bay of Naples: white squid with round black eyes, jet-propelling themselves in murky tanks, bouquets of sea anemones fluttering their fronds, little dogfish of the kind that swallowed Pinocchio. During the war, some famished Neapolitans got in and ate up the collection. In those terrible

*The garden of the Museo Pignatelli is a
tranquil retreat from traffic chaos.*

days, bombed-out families were forced to live in caves behind Santa Lucia (now sealed), where they ate sea snails off the rocks and sent children to beg in the streets.

The park's western end is the Piazza della Repubblica roundabout in the Mergellina district. A few streets beyond, the Porto Sannazzaro is the Mergellina terminus for the ferries and *aliscafi* (hydrofoil) boats that leave every few minutes for the islands of Pozzuoli and Sorrento. Beyond the port is a little park lined with good seafood restaurants, less touristy than those of Santa Lucia. Posillipo's hills close the seafront here.

Just behind the church of Santa Maria di Piedigrotta (past the railway bridge on a curving road to the left of the upper tunnel) is the entrance to a garden — legend has it that Virgil was buried here, although the ancient scribe is known to have died in Brindisi. One can also see the tombstone of the poet Leopardi. The garden is worth visiting for a fine view over the bay.

The Centre

The gateway to Old Naples is the **Via Toledo** as it climbs the hill from the Piazza San Ferdinando and the Royal Palace. It is still marked Via Roma on some street signs and maps.

At the beginning of the Via Toledo, opposite the Galleria Umberto's western entrance, is a station for one of the three funiculars to residential Vomero on the heights. To the left of the Via Toledo is a no-go area for tourists, the Quartiere Spagnoli, where soldiers were billeted during the centuries of Spanish rule. Now it is the base for hit-and-run purse-snatchers, who cruise shopping streets on motor scooters and disappear with their loot into the alleys and staircase streets of this crowded district; tourists should enter *with* caution and *without* valuables, or avoid the area altogether.

From the Via Toledo it is preferable to turn right down the Via Armando Diaz, where fruit-bearing orange trees are planted. A typical example of the boring architecture of Mussolini's fascist era is the Central Post Office in the Piazza Matteotti. In contrast, at the head of the Via Monteoliveto around the corner, is the Renaissance Florentine façade of the **Palazzo Gravina**, now the university's School of Architecture. In preparation for the G7 summit held here in July 1994, major road and monument restoration work was carried out, and the city centre is greatly improved as a result.

Naples has almost 400 churches, some virtually next door to each other. Building and beautifying them has supported a force of artists and artisans in the city down the ages. Regardless of when they were built, the churches tend to look alike,

Songs

Nostalgia and melancholy, sunshine and sea, love and betrayal are the hallmarks of songs that are as Neapolitan as pizza. The greatest Neapolitan singer of them all, Enrico Caruso, included "O sole mio!" and "Santa Lucia," in his concerts, along with operatic arias, and made them familiar worldwide. Folk music of a high order, such songs are a balm for the poverty of the back streets and solace for the emigrant.

Neapolitan singing has an ancient pedigree. Night serenades became such a nuisance to the unromantic trying to sleep that King Frederick II issued a decree in 1221 banning the practice. In the 16th century Neapolitan ditties were popular all over Europe. In the 1700s and 1800s, comic operas flowed from Naples. Then café concerts became the rage.

The festival of Santa Maria di Piedigrotta, a popular church in Mergellina, became a contest for new popular songs in 1876. First prize in 1880 went to "Funiculi, Funicula," celebrating the funicular that had opened on Vesuvius. In 1878 "O sole mio!" won second prize of L.200. Even Elvis recorded that one. Other hits emerged over the years, but the festival declined and disappeared in the 1980s.

since most were redecorated in the florid Baroque style of the 17th and 18th centuries, and after only a modest exposure to galaxies of gilded ceilings, flocks of cherubim, and acres of inlaid marble, most visitors have had enough. Don't give up! A few churches have features not to be missed.

One, across the street from the Palazzo Gravina, is the plain, grey **Sant'Anna dei Lombardi**, notable for Renaissance sculpture in its chapels. The Piccolomini Chapel to the left of the entrance holds two fine works by the Florentine artist Antonio Rosselino—a 1475 marble nativity with lively angels dancing on the stable roof, and the tomb of Maria d'Aragona, a masterpiece of classic sobriety. Look for the remarkably modelled life-sized terracotta figures of Guido Mazzoni's Pieta at the end of a chapel to the right of the main altar. On the right at the rear of the church, the stalls of the old sacristy are beautifully backed with intarsia work, designs in inlaid wood of Neapolitan landscapes and optical illusion "cabinets" of musical instruments.

Two blocks up the facing Calata Trinita Maggiore, the Jesuit church popularly known as the **Gesù Nuovo**, in the piazza of the same name, is the apotheosis of Baroque. The unusual grim façade of black lava studs belonged to a 15th-century princely palace and does not prepare one for the blaze of gold within. The building was converted to a church in 1601 and modified over the next 200 years. The decorative spire in the piazza is a *guglia,* an effusive Neapolitan answer to the obelisks of Rome. There are several in the Old City.

The street crossing the Piazza del Gesù Nuovo has seven names in its east–west course but is best known as the **Spaccanapoli**, the "Split-Naples Street." The district, too, is called Spaccanapoli, and it has been at the heart of Naples since Greek and Roman times. A walk along its length, wandering off into side alleys and squares, is the quintessential

Neapolitan experience. Half-doors, with the upper part open, reveal the tidy interiors of *bassi*, windowless one- or two-room street-level apartments, each of which may be home to a large family. Doorways and the street become an extension of the *bassi* where family members sit on chairs peeling vegetables, playing cards, and conversing in explosive bursts of dialect, their hands in perpetual motion.

Just beyond the Piazza del Gesù Nuovo, to the right, looms the church and monastery of **Santa Chiara**. Its soaring Provençal Gothic nave is a magnificent relic of Angevin Naples, completed in 1328. It, too, was covered with Baroque

plaster and gilt in the 18th century. After American bombs caused a two-day fire that gutted the church in 1943, the pure Gothic lines serendipitously recovered were kept in the post-war restoration. Fortunately the bombs spared the glorious 18th-century majolica cloister (open 8:30 A.M.–12:30 P.M. and 4:00–6:00 P.M.)

On the Spaccanapoli, which here is the Via Benedetto Croce, a few steps lead to the **Piazza San Domenico Maggiore**. In the 13th century St. Thomas

Ancient architecture meets modern day in the Spaccanapoli.

Aquinas taught in the convent attached to the church here. Its *guglia* commemorates the terrible plague of 1656, which carried off half the population.

Turn left at the square, past the imposing portal of the Palazzo di Sangro, and right in the Via F. de Sanctis to find the incredible **Capella Sansevero**—incredible for the sheer volume of decoration in this private chapel and burial place of the di Sangro family, Princes of Sansevero, and for the eccentricities of the 18th-century Prince Raimondo. He can be seen above the inside doorway, climbing out of a tomb, madly waving his sword. In a crypt to the right are two pop-eyed skeletons meshed in metal veins. They are rumoured to be the bodies of servants Raimondo experimented on in an attempt to improve on nature by "metallizing" the circulatory system. Note the remarkable clinging shroud on the alabaster figure of the Dead Christ by Giuseppe Sammartino (1753).

The **Via dei Tribunali**, another former Roman street above the Spaccanapoli, is flanked by a very old arcade. In the morning the street is a market swarming with housewives, who delve into buckets of fish and rifle produce stalls for the best buys.

In **San Lorenzo Maggiore** and its cloister, set back on a platform on the right, excavations have uncovered parts of the Roman law courts and, below that, a Greek shop that did business on this important street of Neapolis. The church has been restored to the Gothic of the French architects who built the luminous ribbed apse in the late 1200s. Note the 14th-century tomb of Catherine of Austria by Tino di Camaino.

The little **Via San Gregorio Armeno** descends here to the Spaccanapoli (Via San Biagio dei Librai now), past the workshops of families who for generations have made hand-painted terracotta Christmas crib figurines called *presepi*. The best, in mid-block, will amaze and delight you with their minute detail. A shoemaker sits at a bench with tiny nails in his mouth, a butcher carves a ham, a fruiterer holds up watermelon slices. If the adjoining church of San Gregorio Armeno is open, duck into its restful cloister, where orange trees surround a graceful fountain.

Il Duomo, officially the **cathedral of San Gennaro**, is one block to the left of the Spaccanapoli intersection with the Via del Duomo. The cathedral is an unfortunate composite of styles dating back to pre-Christian times, if you count the more than 100 Greek and Roman columns incorporated in the 16 piers of its nave. The first Angevin king, Charles I of Anjou, began the cathedral in 1272 on the site of a fifth-century church that in turn had replaced a Roman temple. The oldest portion is actu-

The harmonious cloister of Santa Chiara is a typically Neapolitan extravaganza.

ally another church, Santa Restituta, on a lower level entered from the left aisle. This basilica of the fourth century retains some fifth-century mosaics in the domed baptistery and notable 13th-century marble reliefs in the side chapels.

On the opposite side of the cathedral, the **Cappella di Tesoro** (Treasury Chapel) enshrines the all-important relics of San Gennaro, protector saint of Naples.

Domenichino of Bologna painted most of the 17th-century frescoes in this chapel, despite strong-arm intimidation by local artists who resented an out-of-towner muscling in on their territory. Banded as the "Cabal of Naples," these artists defaced Domenichino's work by night, mugged his servant, and, in another case, contracted for the murder of a non-member.

As the Via del Duomo descends toward the harbour it crosses the Corso Umberto I, one of the city's major arteries. Known as Il Rettifilo because it runs in a straight line from the Piazza G. Bovio to the Piazza Garibaldi, it sliced through the slums of Old Naples in the 1890s as part of the urban clean-up prompted by a cholera epidemic. Three blocks past the intersection, the Via Giubbonari passes under a Gothic clock tower into the **Piazza del Mercato**, with the church of **Santa Maria del Carmine** ahead.

Il Duomo, scene of the bizarre ceremony on which Naples' fortunes supposedly depend.

35

The market square is a mess, but it is laden with history. A headsman's block for condemned nobles and a gallows for commoners were kept in the square—and used—for centuries. In 1647 the fisherman Tommaso Aniello, "Masaniello," began the revolt of the first Parthenopean Republic here. It ended when he was shot nearby. The liberals who proclaimed the abortive second republic in 1799 were executed here, too. Thousands of victims of the 17th-century plague were buried in a common grave under the pavement. Now

The Blood of San Gennaro

Naples has endured so many catastrophes that the populace could be excused for doubting the powers of its patron saint. Nevertheless, twice a year excited crowds gather to see two phials of San Gennaro's congealed blood liquefy and guarantee the city's welfare. Should the miracle fail, or take place too slowly, Naples will be in deep trouble.

The blood is kept under lock and key in the cathedral. On the days of the miracle—the first Saturday in May and 19 September—the archbishop heads a procession from the Treasury Chapel to the main altar. The solidified blood is visible to all in a crystal reliquary tipped from side to side. At the altar it is brought near the saint's head in its silver-gilt effigy. The blood then becomes liquid (usually) and is sometimes seen to "boil." Applause explodes as the archbishop again holds the reliquary high, turns it upside down, and rocks it to show the moving blood within.

Various scientific tests have failed to explain the liquefaction. San Gennaro, Bishop of Benevento, was decapitated for his faith in the arena of Pozzuoli on 19 September, 305. A flask of his blood was collected on the spot by a man whose sight had been miraculously restored by the bishop. The body, head, and flask were buried in the Naples catacombs, kidnapped by Benevento in the Middle Ages, and returned to Naples in 1497. The first documented record of the liquefaction miracle is from 1389. It doesn't always work, and when it doesn't, before long some disaster follows.

the piazza is an arena for the acrobatics of motorbike riders, rearing back to race on one wheel.

The church has a special place in the hearts of Neapolitans. A much venerated 14th-century image of the dark-haired Madonna della Bruna is enshrined here. On 16 July the bell tower erupts in a shower of fireworks cheered by crowds at the church's lively street festival.

> **When visiting churches, shorts, backless dresses, and tank tops should not be worn.**

The inside is nothing special, but note the 14th-century crucifixion. Christ's head is turned to the left instead of the customary right. Legend says this happened in 1493 when a shell hit the church during fighting between the Angevins and Aragonese.

The most colourful outdoor fish market in Naples sprawls along the Via Carmignano, beginning behind the church. It's a crazy scene. Hoses spray octopuses to keep them wriggling, all kinds of crustaceans struggle to escape from their baskets, and the haggling of shoppers competes with the cries of vendors in a fearful din. The street follows the line of old city walls. Through the arch and across the Rettifilo, street stalls of the Forcella market spill over into the alleys around the Via Forcella, where the Spaccanapoli ends. This is the Naples "thieves' market," famous during World War II as the clearing house for loot lifted from the Allied forces. The glamour is gone now, though the crowded streets are fun for photographers. Patient browsing through the second-hand furniture and plain junk might turn up a bargain.

The Piazza Garibaldi is another product of the *sventramento*, the 19th-century "disembowelling" of Old Naples in the interests of sanitation and urban planning. Nevertheless, the district around the square currently has an unsavoury reputation for hustlers and pickpockets. From the modern Central

Railway Station the Circumvesuviana line serves Vesuvius, Pompeii, Herculaneum, and Sorrento. It is both the terminus of trains from Rome and of a metro that runs on the same track. There is a tourist information office in the upper concourse. A new metro from Vomero to the station and the city centre and beyond to Secondigliano is partly completed. It currently runs north from Piazza Vanvitelli to Piazza Medaglie d'Oro and makes seven stops along the line.

A handsome remnant of the old city walls, the Porta Capuana, adorns a plaza down the Via Alessandro Poerio from the Piazza Garibaldi. This is where buses leave every 20 minutes for Caserta. Behind the Vicaria, the Naples courthouse, sidestreets off the Via dei Tribunali, the Spaccanapoli's upper rival, have small surprises for the exploring walker. On a decrepit palazzo up the Via Atri, for example, is a tablet recording the visit of "Volfango" Goethe. In the narrow Vico Purgatorio ad Arco and Vico del Fico al Purgatorio overhead balconies almost touch. Via Tribunali is the place to be from 27–30 September during the San Gaetano street fair.

The Via Tribunali ends shortly before the Porta di Alba, a covered passageway to the Piazza Dante, a green, palm-planted semicircle interrupting the Via Toledo. Several restaurants popular with Neapolitans have terraces on the piazza. The Porta di Alba arcade is devoted to booksellers. Antiques shops abound on the facing Via Santa Maria di Constantinopoli on its way to the Piazza Cavour. In the opposite direction this street becomes Via San Sebastiano, devoted to musical instruments. It crosses the Spaccanapoli at the Piazza Gesù, completing this labyrinthine circuit through Old Naples.

The Heights and the Museums

The upper levels of Naples possess three important museums, a fort, parks, and villas with sweeping views of the city

The Royal Palace at Caserta

The Royal Palace of the Bourbons at Caserta, 28 km (18 miles) northeast of Naples (open 9 a.m.–2 p.m. Monday–Friday, 9 a.m.–1:30 p.m. Saturday–Sunday, closed Monday) was built by Charles III, who almost certainly had Versailles in mind when he set out in 1751 to create the most grandiose palace in Italy. He never had a chance to enjoy his extravagance, for he inherited the throne of Spain and moved to Madrid 15 years before the palace was completed in 1774 by his son, Ferdinand I.

The palace has some 1,200 rooms, 1,790 windows, and 34 staircases. The architect Vanvitelli's masterpiece is the grand staircase of marble and inlaid coloured stone surmounted by a double elliptical vault. Hidden behind the rim of the lower vault, musicians played to greet the king and his guests as they arrived for state receptions. At the top of the stairs Vanvitelli created a theatrical octagonal vestibule of columns, cupolas, and arches. To one side, the gorgeous Palatine Chapel gleams in gold, green, and white. Scarred antique columns along the sides are from the Serapeum of Pozzuoli. To the rear of the second courtyard is another Vanvitelli gem, the Court Theatre.

Facing the front: to the left are the Old Apartments, mostly furnished in Louis XV and XVI styles with damask wall coverings in pastel shades and elaborate Venetian chandeliers. It is difficult to imagine family life in these stiff, museum-like halls. Only the bathrooms seem intimate. There are just two; the one created for Ferdinand and his Maria Carolina has a marble tub lined with gilded bronze and the ultimate in 18th-century luxury—hot and cold water taps. The New Apartments on the other side of the front wing were furnished by Murat with very fine Empire furnishings brought from Paris.

During World War II the palace was the Allied headquarters after 1943. In the high-vaulted white-and-gold Throne Room on 29 April, 1945, British General Harold Alexander accepted surrender of the German army in Italy.

The magnificent park is worth visiting to see the **Cascata Grande**, an immense waterfall tumbling down a wooded hill. Shuttle buses run regularly between the palace and the Fountain of Diana at the foot of the 76-metre (249-foot) Cascade.

and bay. Begin halfway up, at the **Museo Archeologico Nazionale** on the extension of Via Toledo/Via Roma.

This museum's pride is its unsurpassed collection of antiquities. Since 1777 it has brought together treasures from Pompeii, Herculaneum, and Phlegrean Fields sites, as well as the Farnese collection of Roman statues that Charles III of Bourbon inherited from his mother.

There's a lot to see, and it isn't made easier by a never-ending programme of rearranging galleries, irregular schedules when rooms are closed, too many halls of densely crowded statues, poorly displayed exhibits, and explanations only in Italian. Don't be discouraged. The many masterpieces more than compensate for these deficiencies. Here are a few of the best.

The ground floor is mostly devoted to Roman copies of the work of the greatest sculptors of ancient Greece. Many are stiff and stereotyped, but they provide our only notion of masterworks that no longer exist. In Hall I, the two **Tyrannicides**, striding to strike, are copies of a copy made in Athens in 440 B.C. to replace the original, carried off by Persians. Compare this with the refinement and pathos of the Borgia *stele*, an original fifth-century B.C. Greek funerary monument of a man and his dog.

In Hall III the Doryphorus of Polycleitus of Argos, found in Pompeii, is the only complete copy of a statue famous throughout the ancient world as the embodiment of

Volcanic areas such as the Phlegrean Fields emit sulphurous steam.

the ideal male form. In the same hall, the curly-haired figure of Apollo, also from Pompeii, is very fine. But most of the copies are graceless compared to the delicacy of the drapery and natural pose of an original fourth-century B.C. headless Nereid riding a sea monster, in Hall VI. It was one of many artworks taken from Greece as booty by Roman legions.

The highlights of the Farnese collection are the hefty, bulging **Hercules** in Hall XI and the **Farnese Bull** group in Hall XVI. Dirce, the woman under the rearing bull, is being tied to his horns—a rather severe punishment she earned by trying to cheat the two boys out of their inheritance. Both statues were found in the 16th-century excavations of the Baths of Caracalla at Rome. The Bull is a much-restored copy of a sec-

---

"Chiuso!"

Chiuso (pronounced "Kyoo-zo") is a word you'll learn immediately after *grazie* and *per favore*. It means closed. Closed for lunch, closed by a strike, closed "temporarily" for repairs for many years, closed for whatever reasons and for however long, "Who knows, signore?" Your informant hunches his shoulders towards his ears, turns both palms up, and raises his eyebrows in a classic Neapolitan shrug.

Be prepared every day to find something you hoped to see *chiuso*. Numerous rooms in the National Museum have been closed for years; others, and not always the same ones, are closed in the afternoons when the rest of the museum is open. The "new" museum attached to the Herculaneum ruins, beginning to flake and crumble like a ruin itself, is tightly shut. Landmark churches listed on the Naples Tourist Bureau itinerary of artistic monuments are padlocked, or open only a few hours a day. The Vesuvius chair-lift hasn't run since 1984. The Blue Grotto is *chiuso* when wind whips up the waves, closing the narrow entrance. The majority of petrol stations are *chiuso* on Monday. Some that say *aperto* (open) are unstaffed and effectively *chiuso* unless you have the right notes and know how to operate their money machines.

ond-century B.C. work from Rhodes. It is easy to see how such classic figures excited and influenced Renaissance artists.

The mezzanine floor displays the finest mosaics from Pompeii. Exceptional is the large **Battle of Issus** from the House of the Dancing Faun. Alexander the Great charges bareheaded from the left as Persian soldiers try to turn the horses of Darius's chariot for flight. The Faun is here, too. The Nile Scenes and detailed mosaics of marine creatures in the adjoining room are from the same house.

Upstairs, to the right, look for the treasures from the Villa of the Papyri in Herculaneum. This mansion and its garden were a veritable art gallery. The seated young **Mercury** was found there, together with the poised bronze racer and the row of muses that lined the garden pool. The Romans excelled in realistic portrait busts, and the bronze head titled **Pseudo-Seneca** is a superb characterization.

On the left coming from the stairs, don't miss the series of rooms containing domestic items: lamps, mirrors, combs, theatre tickets, shoes, kitchenware, charred food, the instruments from Pompeii's House of the Surgeon, and the beautiful 115-piece silver service from the House of Menander. The top floor, which has been closed in recent times, is given over to a hoard of Greek and Etruscan pottery, as well as the museum's collection of coins from antiquity to the present.

On leaving the museum, turn left past the Piazza Cavour, up the Via Vergini and the connecting Via della Sanita, to one of the city's most typical, untouristy neighbourhoods, the **Quartiere della Sanita**. The roadway is an ant hill of milling shoppers, swerving motor scooters, and shouting vendors. After the winding street passes under Ponte della Sanita, which bridges a thickly populated ravine, there are many *bassi* and small workshops burrowed into the hillside, where high-fashion shoes and gloves sold downtown are made.

The area was a burial ground in antiquity, and there are a number of catacombs here, including the **Catacombe di San Gaudioso**, with skulls embedded in the walls. You have to track down and tip the sacristan of the Santa Maria della Sanita church next to the bridge to get in. More accessible and extensive are the **Catacombe di San Gennaro**. Continue straight up from the National Museum to the domed Madre del Buon Consiglio church where the road doubles back sharply just below Capodimonte. To the left and rear of the church is the ticket booth for the catacombs (open, with a guide, 9:30 to 11:45 A.M. daily). The first tombs cut into the rock here were for second-century noble Roman families. Use by Christians probably began a century or so later. The arched halls and rooms on two levels are decorated with very early mosaics and frescoes (Christ is represented without a beard).

Crowning the hill at the end of Via Capodimonte, the street that began as Via Toledo, the park of the **Palazzo Reale di Capodimonte** is an oasis of calm and fresh air. The usual boring palace chambers, of which Naples has more than enough, have been stripped and re-arranged as a modern gallery—and a truly choice one it is, containing the Farnese art collection, together with works of art, porcelain, and armour from other museums and churches in the city.

Recent restoration brought out the brilliant colours of Masaccio's *Crucifixion* and uncovered the "tree of life"

Balloons provide an unexpected burst of colour on this Neapolitan street.

on the cross. This is part of a set of panels now divided among museums in Pisa, Berlin, London, and Vienna. Botticelli's *Madonna and Child, with Angels*, is an early Renaissance treasure. The *Transfiguration* of Giovanni Bellini, flooded with light, is one of the master's most important works. Look for Lorenzo Lotto's *Portrait of Archbishop De Rossi*.

In the room devoted to Titian, note the crafty look of *Pope Paul III* facing a fawning Farnese nephew. There's an interesting portrait of the young emperor *Charles V* by Bernart van Orley. In the same room, note the grotesque crowd about to stone the *Woman Taken in Adultery*, by Lucas Cranach, and the superb *Adoration of the Magi* tryptich of Joos van Cleve.

Next comes the wonderful *Blind Leading the Blind* of Pieter Breughel and, by the same master, a curious *Misanthrope* in which a thief cuts the miser's purse in the shape of the world. Guido Reni is represented by a fat *Atalanta* racing a trim Hippomenes—one wouldn't have thought he needed to drop golden apples to slow her down. An incredibly merry *Judith* with the head of Holofernes turns out to be by a female Neapolitan painter, Artemisia Gentileschi, perhaps making an early feminist statement.

The **Vomero** district is on another hill, reached from the seafront and centre of Naples by funicular. The three stations are at the foot of Via Toledo, on Piazza Montesanto across the Via Toledo from the Piazza Dante, and in the Chiaia district at Piazza Amedeo. The Montesanto funicular comes closest to the **Castel Sant'Elmo**, but they all arrive within close walking distance of each other.

The citadel of Naples, the castle is a sombre and brooding presence when seen from below, but a breeze-swept platform for admiring the view when on its Piazza d'Armi. King Robert of Anjou built the first castle on this strategic spot in 1328.

Just below the castle, the **Certosa di San Martino**, a sumptuously Baroque former Carthusian monastery, houses the **Museo Nazionale di San Martino**. Neapolitans love this museum because it is all about *them*—their history, customs, costumes, and the royal reminders of the time when Naples was the capital of a kingdom. Their children love it, too, for the most colourful of all Christmas cribs and for walks in its gardens hung above the city. The museum is open 9:00 A.M. to 2:00 P.M. Tuesday to Sunday, but is closed all day Monday. The collection has been extensively rearranged, which in the past meant many galleries were unpredictably closed. However, all galleries are now open to the public.

From the cloistered entry, skip the pompous gold coach and pass right out to the terraced gardens of vines, pines, and paths. From the balcony you'll be able to identify the main landmarks of the city, spread out like a map below. To the right of the little cloister, the Maritime Section exhibits ship models. On the left, steps go down to the **Presepe Cuciniello**. This must be the champion of all Neapolitan cribs—Bethlehem is pure 18th-century Campania. Each of the 177 painted terracotta figures is a genuine character, an exquisite work of art by the popular sculptor Giuseppe Sammartino, and clothed in handsewn period costumes.

Rooms around the main cloister are devoted to the paintings of Neapolitan artists, costumes, glassware, and historical exhibits. The Belvedere room in the southeast corner of the monastery has an unusual view embracing the Campanian plain, Vesuvius, and the bay.

The cloister is a restrained, rather Florentine construction, with a small cemetery in one corner. Proceed directly through the chapter room of the monastery's church to see the very fine intarsia work on stalls and cabinets in the Sacristy and, in the Treasury Chapel, *Descent from the Cross* by José Ribera.

The church is best seen by entering from the outer courtyard. San Martino's monastery was founded in 1325 by the Angevin dynasty, but it was entirely done over in Baroque in the 16th and 17th centuries. The original Gothic arch can be discerned over the altar, now filled with a very busy crucifixion scene.

Dozens of Neapolitan-school painters worked on these walls and on the side chapels, and Ribera's prophets fill spaces over the chapel arches. Note the richly inlaid pavements. The balustrade, with inlaid doves eating grapes in agate, lapis lazuli, and other semi-precious stones, is by Sammartino, who sculpted the Christmas crib.

The centre of the Vomero is the **Piazza Vanvitelli**. All the main streets up here are named after artists, architects, and composers, a custom which was intended to add sophistication to the district as it developed in the late 19th century by the middle class escaping the lower echelons of the city.

A block to the left of the Via A. Scarlatti from the Piazza, on the Via Cimarosa, the **Villa Floridiana** occupies a large, wooded preserve that is the Vomero's public park. The villa houses the **Museo Nazionale della Ceramica "Duca di Martina,"** whose collection includes not only porcelain from the royal Capodimonte factory but also a valuable selection of Meissen, Sèvres, Nymphenburg, Wedgwood, and Oriental ceramics and majolica. It is open from 9:00 A.M. to 2:00 P.M. Tuesday through Saturday and 9:00 A.M. to 1:00 P.M. onSunday. During August and September it is also open on Monday and closes at 8:00 P.M. on Tuesday, Thursday, and Saturday.

OUTLYING AREAS

Posillipo and Fuorigrotta

Long before the Vomero became fashionable, Posillipo was the retreat of the rich of Naples. Monte Posillipo, rimmed with apartment buildings and villas, drops gently to the sea, closing the western end of the inner bay. The Via di Posillipo around this cape was begun by Murat in 1812 as a more direct route to Pozzuoli.

This panoramic road follows the shore from Mergellina and climbs past parks and faded princely estates, such as the 17th-century **Palazzo di Donn'Anna**, to the left on the coast. Passing a park with a memorial to World War I soldiers, the road reaches a crest at the Quadrivio del Capo crossroads. Take the left road down about a kilometre to **Marechiaro**. Popular seafood and pizza restaurants ring the tiny harbour-side piazza of this animated fishing village, made famous by Tosti's haunting song of the same name.

The port of Pozzuoli was of great economic significance in Roman times.

Just beyond the Quadrivio, the Parco Virgiliano's belvedere offers splendid views over the bay out to Capri.

The lump of an islet below is Nisida, connected by a causeway to the ugly factories of Bagnoli. The Posillipo escarpment is part of the wall of another volcanic crater. The road descends here toward Pozzuoli, past the recently restored **Parco Archeologico Pausilypon**. This park contains many interesting remains, as well as a tunnel carved through the hill of Posillipo to the villa of a Roman politician.

Posillipo's ridge is pierced by parallel tunnels from Piedigrotta that connect with the *tangenziale* ring road around Naples in the populous Fuorigrotta suburb. Just beyond the tunnels is a supreme monument of modern Naples, the San Paolo football stadium. The 85,000-seat stadium was one of the sites of the 1990 World Cup.

In Fuorigrotta, trade fairs are held at the extensive Mostra d'Oltremare exhibition grounds. Nearby, the Edenlandia amusement park has a variety of rides, fairytale castles, and boating and food stands in a setting of greenery.

Pozzuoli and the Phlegrean Fields

In the days of Imperial Rome the fashionable place to have a vacation villa was along the northern curve of the Bay of Naples called the Phlegrean Fields (*Campi Flegrei*), from the Greek words meaning "burning fields." In fact, the whole district overlies volcanic fire, dotted with hot springs and 13 small craters, one of which still shoots up clouds of sulphurous steam. Although stripped over the centuries and half buried by neglect, the remains of the Roman playground can still easily be recreated in the mind's eye as a Hollywood-style extravaganza.

The town of Pozzuoli, 13 km (8 miles) from Naples, is the centre for visiting the Phlegrean Fields sites. On a rise behind the harbour, the Duomo, the **Cattedrale de San Procolo**, was just another 17th-century church until a fire in 1964 uncovered the marble walls and cornices of a temple to Augustus, the first emperor to be deified. The composer Pergolesi, who died in Pozzuoli in 1736, is buried here. These days, the town's most famous native is Sophia Loren.

Set back from the port area in a park are the sunken ruins of the **Serapeum**, a first-century A.D. covered market (*macellum*), whose grand design suggests the wealth of Puteoli, as Pozzuoli was known in Roman times. Of special scientific interest are the three large columns at the rear. They have been eaten away by sea snails some 3 to 5 metres (11 to 18 feet) from the base, as a result of bradyseism, a rising and sinking of the land that for a time partially submerged the market, then raised it. This process continues. The once-flooded market floor lifted nearly a metre (3 feet) during tremors in 1970 and is now slowly subsiding again. All along the Gulf of Pozzuoli out to its tip at Cape Miseno the sea covers Roman buildings that once stood on the shore. It's a great treasure-hunting ground for divers.

The **Amphitheatre** of Puteoli (open 9:00 A.M. to 4:00 P.M.) is reached by steps and a short street on the far side of the railway station opposite the harbour. It was largely covered by volcanic material until the 19th century and, as a result, you can see almost intact the behind-the-scenes network for staging gladiatorial combats—corridors, ramps, and stalls for wild animals under the arena floor, and the square openings where their cages were hoisted to the surface. Built in the first century A.D., the amphitheatre held 35,000 spectators, and could be flooded for mock naval battles.

The Solfatara, about ten minutes' walk from the amphitheatre, is a shallow moonscape crater filled with glaring white ash. You are walking atop a snoozing volcano, with the stink of sulphur in the air from steaming fumaroles (vents emitting hot gases) and bubbling mud pits. Fences and "Danger!" signs keep you to a path around the 2.5 km (1½ mile) perimeter. At the Boca Grande fumarole, steam temperatures are over 160°C (320°F). This is where guides light a match at a vent, causing clouds of white ionized vapour to puff from cracks nearby.

Baia and Cuma

The seaside village of **Baia** was once ancient Baiae, a luxurious holiday resort for wealthy Romans. The **Parco Archeologico** encloses the grandiose ruins of the Imperial Palace and baths, but signposting is confusing, in typical Neapolitan style, and the entrance is virtually concealed. The easiest way is a footbridge over the tracks at the railway station. In the park (open 9:00 A.M. to 4:00 P.M.) very little is signposted, and then the popular names are inaccurate, but never mind. The site, on a cliff with three terrace levels, commands a view over the sea from Cape Miseno on the right on to the Sorrento shore, Monte Faito, Vesuvius, Posillipo, and Pozzuoli to the left. The Imperial Palace, called the **Terme di Baia**, was built and added to by the Caesars over 400 years from the first century A.D. Up and down the coast were the villas of notables—Julius Caesar, Lucullus, Pompey, Cicero, Sulla—a veritable Miami Beach of the rich and famous. Many of these villas are now under water up to 500 metres (545 yards) offshore, thanks to bradyseism (see page TK). Others provide walls for houses on the main street between the cliff and the bay. The whole complex was raided and looted by Saracens in the 800s.

Tiberius left Capri to die on this coast in 37 A.D. and was succeeded by the psychopath Caligula, who built a bridge of boats joining Baiae with Puteoli. Nero was in residence in 59

The 16th century castle at Baia was built by the Spanish viceroy Pedrio de Toledo.

A.D., when, having failed to drown his mother in a staged boating accident, he had her stabbed in her beach house. Hadrian died here in 138 A.D.

At the foot of the cliff was once a large pool, now a garden connected by an arcade to the "Temple of Mercury," actually a huge domed bath, now flooded, with a terrific echo. Try clapping your hands. The "Temple of Diana," half a dome like a bandstand, behind the railroad station, and the romantic "Temple of Venus," with trees growing from its roof, across the road by the harbour, were also parts of the thermal establishment.

After Baia the road climbs inland past the frowning block of a fort built by the Spanish in the 16th century as a defence against the Saracens. Descending to Bacoli, look for signs to the **Piscina Mirabile** at the far end of town on the Via A.

Greco. This vast covered reservoir carved out of the rock, the largest of its kind, was the terminus of an aqueduct, designed to provide water for the Roman fleet at Miseno.

Pliny the Elder was in command of the fleet here when Vesuvius erupted in 79 A.D., and met his death trying to save fugitives from Pompeii. The famous description of the event by his nephew Pliny the Younger was made from this vantage point. For a very special 360-degree view of the coast, bay, islands, and volcanic profile of the Phlegrean Fields, cross the harbour and drive up to the Cape Miseno lighthouse.

The holy of holies of the Phlegrean Fields was at **Cuma**, about 9 km (5½ miles) from Bacoli, past a sandy bathing beach, the Marinadi Fusaro, and Torregaveta, the end of the line on the Cumana railway. Cuma became an important city that founded Neapolis (Naples) in the seventh century B.C. and controlled the Phlegrean Fields region for nearly 500 years, its decline under the Romans. Statues were found in the 19th and 20th centuries and archaeological digs began. The acropolis is now in a fenced park (open 9:00 A.M. to 4:00 P.M., closed Mondays) surrounded by farmland studded with ruins, including an amphitheatre.

This is the site of the famous **Cave of the Cumaean Sybil**, who answered questions and foretold the future, for a fee. People came from afar to consult the Sybil and her successors. The cave, which was enlarged with chambers, is approached through a long and spooky keyhole-shaped tunnel lit by windows cut in the hillside.

From the Sybil's cave a Via Sacra paved by the Romans climbs to the ruins of a temple to Apollo and then to the heights, site of a temple to Jupiter, later converted to a Christian church. Not much remains of these structures, layered in platforms of stone laid over a thousand years by successive inhabitants. Nevertheless, the entire precinct has a mysterious aura.

The old Via Domiziana from Cuma toward Pozzuoli passes under the **Arco Felice**, an arched defile 20 metres (65 feet) high cut in the rock by the Romans in the first century A.D. This leads to a turnoff to Exit 14, the end of the *tangenziale* superhighway from Naples, which can be reached at the Fuorigrotta exit in 15 minutes. On the outskirts of Naples is **Agnano Terme**, the main thermal spa of the area and geologically a part of the Phlegrean Fields. The spa buildings, offering a range of temperatures in steam rooms and glorious mud, are in a crater. A day trip from Naples to this area can easily be managed without a car. The Cumana line from the Montesanto Station stops at the principal sites all the way out to Cuma. The whole area is great for walkers; many of the most beautiful corners and curious archaeological remains are accessible only on foot.

ERUPTIVE SIGHTS

Pompeii

The grandeur and decay of most Roman monuments make the Romans themselves seem as remote to us as Babylonians. Five minutes in Pompeii will change all that. The imme-

A daunting entrance to the Cave of the Cumaean Sybil.

diacy of the human touch is overwhelming. Here are the houses, businesses, shopping streets, bakeries, theatres, and bars where people lived lives not so different from our own —until disaster struck.

What happened to the 20,000 citizens of Pompeii on 24 August, 79 A.D., was not as sudden as a bomb blast, but just as devastating. There had been warnings, and a bad earthquake 17 years earlier. Tremors shook the earth for several days in late August. Then around noon on the 24th a mushroom cloud shot up from Vesuvius. The mountain was green to its crest with vineyards and had never been considered threatening.

Soon the cloud obscured the sun, and, out of the darkness and growing stench of gas, the ashes, cinders, and pumice pebbles called *lapilli* fell steadily. The earth shuddered repeatedly and tidal waves dashed in from the sea. Terrified people fled, on foot and by boat. The roofs of buildings collapsed under the weight of volcanic debris. For three days it continued. When the sky cleared on 27 August Pompeii was buried under 7 metres (23 feet) of ash. This light material solidified with rain and time, preserving everything it encased as if in a time capsule—an entire city and everything that was in it on that fateful day, intact down to the most humble and intimate details.

Pompeii remained hidden until 1594, when workmen tunnelling for an aqueduct unearthed some walls and

The ruins of Cuma, once a great and powerful Greek city.

tablets. Serious excavations were begun under the Bourbons in 1748, and most of the statues and valuables were removed in the next 150 years. Some had already been recovered by their owners, digging in the ashes right after the eruption. Much of the treasure is in the National Museum in Naples (see Pompeii first, then your museum visit will be even more rewarding). Digging continues when funds are available, and so far about four-fifths of Pompeii has been uncovered.

The city thus revealed was a prosperous commercial seaport at the mouth of the Sarno River. The sidestreets were full of bars and brothels. The most prominent citizens were newly rich merchants who built and decorated showy houses to boost their egos (the Imperial court and Roman aristocrats had their vacation villas at fashionable Stabia, Herculaneum, Neapolis, or near Baiae, across the bay). The bulk of Pompeii's population consisted of working people, artisans, shopkeepers, and slaves.

Traces of several pre-Roman cultures are found in Pompeii, which retained a strong ethnic flavour. Graffiti in several languages abound, including political campaign slogans, ads for current entertainments, or scribbles of the "Gaius loves Flavia" variety. Some have a rebellious ring, such as "Share out all the public money, say I." It was a boisterous, crass, cosmopolitan city of secondary importance at the time, but incomparably precious today through the accident of its preservation.

This book does not attempt to describe or even list all the fascinating features of Pompeii, and you may find a complete guidebook to the site helpful. What follows covers a ramble of a day, including a lunch stop at the Punto di Restoro cafeteria, and highlights the major sites.

Visits begin at the **Porta Marina**, the sea gate, one of eight in the city walls, separating 14 watchtowers. Actually there are two gates tunnelled here, one for pedestrians and one for the

*The raised paving stones on this street form
the Roman equivalent of a pedestrian crossing.*

carts that brought loads up from the docks below on to the Via
Marina. Its lava paving stones, like all the streets of Pompeii,
are rutted by the passage of cart and chariot wheels.

Across the street is the **Temple of Apollo**, built by Samnites. The sundial on the pillar to the left of the raised temple
is a reminder of Apollo's role as god of the sun. Originals of
the facing bronze statues of Apollo and his sister, Diana, god-
dess of the moon and the hunt, are in the National Museum.

A few steps more and you are in the **Forum**, a spacious
meeting place once lined with a two-storey arcade. Pompeii's
central plaza would be the envy of many a town its size today.
Stones blocked traffic from entering. The principal religious,
administrative, and commercial centres were all nearby. Imagine it glistening white, filled with the statues whose bases dot
the area and thronged with shoppers, idlers, and crowds listen-
ing to political speeches or attending religious ceremonies.

At the head of the Forum stands the raised **Temple of
Jupiter**. To its right, the central market, the **Macellum**, originally domed, is divided into stalls for produce vendors and

the *argentari*, moneychangers. Looming over all, straight ahead, is Vesuvius, far from dead and suddenly looking ominous. It's bound to erupt again some day!

When the disaster struck, many Pompeiians were overcome by poisonous fumes. The wet ash solidified around their bodies like a mould that emptied in time as the flesh decomposed. By filling these "moulds" with plaster, archaeologists have created lifelike casts of the victims. Several of these are to be seen in the **Horreum**, a sort of shed for storing and weighing grain now stocked with wine jars and crockery, to the left of the Temple of Jupiter. A man crouches, covering his face with his hands. A pregnant woman lies face down.

The **Suggestum**, a tribune for orators, occupies the middle of the arcade on the west side. Across the Forum are several small temples, including one to Vespasian, the emperor who introduced public toilets (there is one at number 28 on the west side). The buildings on the south end of the Forum served as the "City Hall," offices of the municipal council and other dignitaries.

After you see the Forum, there is no obvious itinerary to follow in Pompeii. The orderly Roman rectilinear layout of blocks and streets has been divided by archaeologists into numbered Regions, Insulae (blocks), and houses, but the system is incomplete, changing, and can be confusing to the uninitiated. Start with the **Terme del Foro**, small baths whose entrance is beyond the cafeteria and left on Via delle Terme.

Visiting the baths was an important part of the daily routine of these Romans. First comes the vaulted "locker room," lined with seats and niches for clothes. Off this are the *frigidarium*, for cooling off after the *tepidarium*, where a brazier heated the air, and the *caldarium,* with a pool and steam from an external boiler. Exercising was done in the adjoining gym, or *palestra,* and there were separate facilities for women. Note the delicate stucco work on the ceilings. The cast of a body found here was that of a slave, identified by the belt that slaves were obliged to wear.

After a healthy workout, the bather could cross the street to a tavern, choosing wine from jars set in the counter. Down the street in the **House of the Tragic Poet**, a much-copied mosaic in the pavement just inside the doorway warns "Beware of the Dog"—*Cave Canem*. Next comes one of Pompeii's largest villas, the many-columned **House of Pansa**. Turn left down the Via Consolare past a fountain embossed with an eagle catching a rabbit and a bakery with three conical stones of grey lava for grinding grain. Surgical instruments displayed in the National Museum were found in the **House of the Surgeon** a bit farther on.

The street descends after leaving the walls at the triple-arched Porta Ercolano and becomes a tree-shaded, romantic lane lined by imposing tombs. Many bear traces of painted and mosaic decoration. At the lane's end, to the left, is the **Villa of Diomedes**. Unusual for Pompeii are the big windows, which must have made this a sunny house, with pleasant views of the large garden. The body of the owner was found with the garden gate key in his hand and, beside him, a slave carrying a bag of valuables.

At this point you leave the ruins proper and can follow the signs on your right to the **Villa of the Mysteries**. This elegant residence is decorated with the largest and most remarkable wall paintings surviving from Roman times. A sequence of scenes on a glowing red background follows the initiation of a newly married woman into the Dionysian mysteries, an orgiastic rite of Greek origin.

The most interesting houses are in the area northeast of the Forum. Return to the crossroads above the Temple of Jupiter and follow the Via della Fortuna. The second block on the left is entirely taken up by the **House of the Faun** and its gardens. Here was an owner with taste, so much so that most of the house's treasures, such as the mosaic of Alexander in a battle scene and the popular dancing faun for which the house is named, are in the National Museum. Even so, the graciousness of the arrangements is notable. There were four dining rooms, one for each season. The coloured marble pavement resembles the design of a patchwork quilt.

Continue another block and turn left into the Vicolo dei Vettii, and Pompeii's most famous house, the **Casa dei Vettii**. Carefully restored, it gives a good idea of how wealthy merchants lived. Paintings in the dining and sleeping rooms done not long before the eruption show cupids engaged in typical activities of the town. Just inside the entrance is a fresco of

Public fountains such as this stood at all major crossroads in Pompeii.

Priapus, god of fertility, weighing his huge penis on a scale against a bag of gold. It used to be covered by a locked panel, and guards made a good income by giving visitors a peek. Now it's out in the open—no longer obscene, just ridiculous. All over Pompeii you'll see phallic signs on houses. These were to ward off the evil eye, similar to the red coral or plastic amulets worn today in southern Italy.

Follow the Vicolo dei Vettii back to the Via della Fortuna and cross to descend the Vico Storto. Note the large bakery with mills on the left. Grain was poured in the top cylinder turned by donkeys or slaves. Wind around to the left on Via degli Augustali to the Vicolo degli Lupanare. Here some businesslike pornography illustrates the services offered in a rather cramped two-storey brothel, the **Lupanar Africani et Victoris**. Across the street, the doorway motto of the **House of Siricus** sums up Pompeii's parvenu creed: *Salve Lucru*—"Hail Money!"

Pompeii's largest baths, the **Terme Stabianae**, occupy nearly a block at the end of this street, with the entrance on the

A cupid hides in an aged fountain at the Casa dei Vettii.

broad Via dell'Abbondanza. To the right of the portal is the men's section with a locker room, a circular, domed cold room, and warm and hot rooms decorated with stucco friezes. Beyond, in the women's baths, the remains of the boiler room and the air space in the walls and floor where steam and hot air circulated can be seen. In the pillar-lined open-air *palaestra* exercise yard note the two bowling courts, perhaps the ancestor of the Italian *bocci* game of bowls. There's a large swimming pool here and a communal latrine.

Across the Via Abbondanza to the right, follow the Via dei Teatri to the **Triangular Forum**, one of the city's earliest sacred precincts, and to two theatres. A gateway leads into the forum, flanked by a long row of columns and shaded by old ilex and cypress trees. It's a quiet and restful spot, especially welcome on a hot day. At the rear, from the base of a sixth-century B.C. Doric temple, there's a good view across the Sarno River's clogged stream to modern Pompeii, Monte Faito, and the Lattari range of the Sorrento peninsula.

The **Teatro Grande** could seat 5,000 people, and is used today for concerts and performances. The iron brackets are used to add wooden benches. In antiquity spectators were shielded from the sun by cloth awnings. The adjoining **Teatro Piccolo** was originally roofed as a concert hall. A plaque reminded the-

A fresco at the Casa dei Vettii is worn by time.

atregoers that "Claudio C.F. Marcello, Patrono" helped pay for the structure. Most of Pompeii's public buildings were erected at the expense of rich citizens, who were often also vote-seeking politicians.

Beyond the large theatre is a colonnaded exercise field and the **Barracks of the Gladiators**. Sixty-four bodies were found inside, some in chains, along with a rich store of weapons and armour, now in the National Museum. Behind the theatres is a small Temple of Isis, for an Egyptian cult with followers in this melting-pot community.

Returning by the Via Stabiana to the Via dell'Abbondanza, turn right and follow it into the area of the **Nuovi Scavi**, the "new" excavations begun in 1911. This is a district of small industries, shops, taverns, hotels, and the villas of a few wealthy businessmen. An effort has been made to reconstruct these premises and to leave some of their contents in place, including casts of bodies found here. Most Pompeiian houses were two-storeyed, but the upper floors were crushed by the weight of ash. Here, many have been restored. Look for fine mosaic floors, stucco, and painted wall decorations and the trappings of artisans and shopkeepers. Many graffiti are protected by glass along the street.

In a laundry, the **Fullonica Stephani** at number 7 on the south side of Insula VI, vats for washing, dyeing, and bleaching occupy the rear. A press stands to the left of the entry, where clothes were handed in through a window in the door. The upper floor held lodgings. Across the way, note the depth of ash filling buildings still unexcavated. Around the corner to the right on this block are the **House of the Underground Portico**, where many bodies were found in the wine cellar, and the elegant **House of Menander**. A collection of exquisite silverware, now in the Naples museum, was unearthed here. In the rear there's a chariot and the skeleton of a horse.

On the north side of the Via dell'Abbondanza, the **Thermopolion of Asellina** is a very well-preserved bar. Note graffiti advertising the names and attractions of prostitutes available in the upstairs cribs. One of the finest houses in this district, with a large bronze-studded door, belonged to Loreius Tibertinus and is notable for its handsome garden.

At the end of the street, the **Villa of Julia Felix** takes up most of the block. It was apparently a hotel, for there are "rooms for rent" signs on the walls. It had its own baths, a large garden, and shops. Behind this villa is the **Amphitheatre**, the oldest surviving in Italy. To the west, the **Large Palaestra** is a vast exercise field 100 metres (109 yards) square, enclosed on three sides by a covered portico and by pines and plane trees. Roots of the original trees were found, enabling archaeologists to recreate the planting.

Pompeii may be reached by the *autostrada* in 20 minutes, once you get outside Naples—which is easier said than done. There are frequent trains to the ruins from the Central Station at the Piazza Garibaldi. Your hotel or the tourist information office can advise you on where to sign up for a guided tour by bus.

Herculaneum

Herculaneum isn't just a smaller Pompeii. It was a very different sort of city in 79 A.D., and the manner of its destruction has left us very different ruins. Whereas Pompeii was big, crass, and bumptious, Herculaneum was small, refined, and patrician. While Pompeii was crushed under falling volcanic debris, Herculaneum was filled from the bottom up by ash and pumice carried on a torrent of ground-hugging superheated gas. Roofs did not cave in. The city was simply inundated by a flood that covered it to an average depth of 20 metres (65 feet). This muck cooled and hardened to encase and protect balconies, furniture, food on the tables, and even glass window panes and wax writing tablets. Once discovered, the material was relatively easy to carve out, a kind of tufa sandstone.

The ruins of Herculaneum have yielded far more treasures of artistic value than Pompeii, although only a fraction of the city has been explored. The difficulty for archaeologists is the fact that another town, Resina, recently renamed Ercolano, sits on top of the site. Little progress has been made since the main sites were uncovered between 1927 and 1962.

The first excavations were made in the 18th and 19th centuries, and did almost as much damage as Vesuvius. Workmen cut trenches and tunnels right through villas and public buildings, hacking away and pulling out loot without making a plan or keeping records of where items were found.

You enter Herculaneum through a gate at the foot of Ercolano's main street, the Corso Ercolano, straight down from the railway station and *autostrada* exit. At Cardo III on the left is the large **House of Argus**, with rather Egyptian-looking columns. On past the intersection of the *decumanus inferior* are the **Forum Baths**, with men's and women's sections built around an exercise court. A Neptune whose legs turn into sea serpents decorates the mosaic floor of the *tepidarium*. Sea creatures painted on the ceiling over the cold plunge were reflected in its water.

East on the *decumanus* at the corner of Cardo IV is the much-photographed **Samnite House**. The Samnites preceded the Romans here, as in Pompeii, and the house is a dignified structure of the second century B.C., one of the oldest in Herculaneum. Diagonally across the intersection, the overhanging roof, beams, and door frame of the **House of the Wooden Partition** are original. Inside, note the cleverly hinged doors that slide on bronze grooves to close off the atrium. A perfectly preserved wooden bed stands in the corner of an adjoining bedroom. A loaf of bread with a bite taken out of it was found in the dining room off the garden where lunch was being served as the disaster struck.

On the east side of Cardo IV above the Samnite House are the **Weaver's House**, the **House of the Charred Furniture**, the **House of the Neptune Mosaic,** and the **House of the Beautiful Courtyard**, all remarkably preserved, with homely bits of everyday belongings, finely fashioned furniture, mosaics, and frescoes. Some may be locked, but a guard with the key shouldn't be far away.

This street ends at a broad pedestrian mall called the *decumanus maximus* and the edge of the still unexcavated Forum under the modern town. **The Palaestra of Hercula-**

Excavation is nowhere near completion at The Palaestra Herculaneum.

neum, which extends under the path from the ticket booth, is only partly uncovered. Tunnellers bashed it badly in 1750, and the high vaulted ceiling of stars on a blue background collapsed. In the centre a cross-shaped pool was fed by water from a bronze serpent coiled around a tree. Apparently games were in progress on the day of the eruption; stone "shot-put" balls were found in the Palaestra.

The finest houses, at the end of Cardo V, had a view over the sea towards Capri from the embankment overlooking Herculaneum's marina. The grandest is the **House of the Deer**, where a pair of delicate sculptures of stags attacked by dogs was found. Neighbours to the left occupied the **House of the Mosaic Atrium**, with its black-and-white chequerboard pavement that rippled under the shock of the eruption.

Herculaneum

Until 1980 only a few bodies had been found in the ruins of Herculaneum, and it was believed that the estimated 5,000 inhabitants had managed to flee to safety. In 1980 hundreds of skeletons of men, women, and children who had taken shelter in vaults at the marina were found.

These skeletons provided a rare opportunity to study the size and health of typical individuals, for Romans cremated their dead and cemeteries contain only urns with ashes. Men were on average 1.65 metres (5 feet 7 inches) tall, while women were considerably shorter. Teeth cavities were uncommon, perhaps because Romans did not have refined sugar in their diets.

Romans enjoyed a level of health care not again available until relatively modern times. A kit of instruments found in the House of the Surgeon in Pompeii included scalpels, forceps, catheters, implements for brain and eye surgery, suction cups, scissors, pincers, and clamps.

This house had glassed-in porticos and a solarium looking out to sea.

Steps at the end of Cardo V descend to the small **Suburban Baths**. Light filters into rooms through windows that once were glassed. The atmosphere is steamy, as befits a bath, because this area is now below sea level and has to be pumped out to prevent flooding. The tubs, tanks, boilers, and even firewood for furnaces have been left as they were found. A frieze of warriors modelled in stucco decorates the dressing room above marble benches. Panelled wooden doors hang on their original hinges. A heavy marble basin lies on its side where it was tossed by the heaving earth. At the end of a corridor, graffiti in a room for private parties tot up the bill for an order of cakes and record the pleasures of a homosexual encounter.

As you climb the steps to leave this small, elegant city brought back from its grave after so many centuries, look behind you. The cone of brooding Vesuvius rises over the rooftops, only 7 km (4½ miles) away.

Vesuvius

Seen from Naples, it is clear that the perfect cone of Vesuvius is actually a volcano within another, much larger volcano. The crater of the mother mountain, Monte Somma, rings Vesuvius to the left, its slope broken off in an eruption 17,000 years ago. The present 1,276-metre (4,173-foot) cone has

Neptune and Amphitrite are shown in this ancient mosaic panel.

grown and changed shape through countless eruptions, the most recent in 1944.

The paved road from Torre del Greco ends some 275 metres (900 feet) below the volcano's rim. Then a half-hour walk up a fairly steep path in the loose reddish cinders brings you to the top (ticket booth open 9:00 A.M. to one hour before sunset). Good walking shoes are essential for this hike, but if you haven't brought any, shoes and staffs can be hired in the car park. In summer, the stream of visitors climbing and descending is continuous.

Around the crater's edge, where wisps of steam drift from fumaroles, intrepid tourists pose for photos. Landslides have partially filled the inner cavity like sands running out of an hourglass. The crater is 200 metres (654 feet) deep and 600 metres (1,962 feet) across. Souvenir kits of a few of the 230-odd minerals the volcano has thrust up from the earth's innards are sold at a stand.

It is certain that Vesuvius will blow its top again one of these days, but it appears now to have entered a predicted cycle of inactivity after erupting every few years since 1858. A 130-year period of inactivity preceded the calamitous eruption of 1631, when 3,000 people were killed, the mountain lost its top, and ashes fell as far away as Istanbul. There were also spectacular eruptions in 1872, 1906, 1929, 1933, and 1944.

The 1944 explosion was preceded by earthquakes; then a stream of superheated lava roared down the Atrio del Cavallo, the valley between Vesuvius and Somma, travelling at a speed of 162 km/h (100 mph). The approach road skirts this lava flow. It is surprising how quickly vegetation creeps back to cover the desolation—in spring the lower slopes are covered with golden broom. In winter the cone often gets a dusting of snow.

ISLAND PARADISES

Capri

The breathtaking beauty of Capri lives up to its legendary claims. Your anticipation builds from the moment you see the island, so tantalizingly close in the centre of the Bay of Naples horizon, yet so intriguingly indistinct in detail. As your boat brings you closer, the island seems to rise out of the sea. Now you see that it is two sheer bluffs of rock joined in the middle by a lower, sloping saddle where white buildings cluster and spill down towards the harbour.

At the **Marina Grande**, ferries come and go constantly amid much flinging of ropes and shouting on the dock. From here you can also join an excursion out to the *Tritone* submarine, for an unusual visit down into the depths of the sea of Capri.

You can take a cab or bus to the Piazza Umberto I, better known as the **Piazzetta**, the town square above, but there is a better way—walk across the quay to the funicular and go up in a cable car, climbing steeply past orchards of figs and lemons and colourful gardens. The terrace of Capri town provides one of many spectacular views of the island. From here you can look down on to the harbour and across the bay. To the left, Anacapri is perched on the massive gray limestone block of Monte Solaro; to the right is Monte Tiberio, the eyrie from which Tiberius ruled the Roman Empire. Straight ahead is Vesuvius and the palisades of Sorrento and its cape.

If the terrace is Capri's balcony, the Piazzetta is its salon. The intimate little square is enclosed on three sides by cafés, bars, and shops, and on the fourth by steps to the church of Santo Stefano. This is the place to buy papers at the corner kiosk, have a second breakfast or an apéritif, and sit watching the world go by. The Piazzetta is packed with umbrella-shaded tables. There are no cars in the town proper—the lanes and alleys are far too narrow—but small electric tractors can get through to carry provisions to shops and hotels, as well as luggage. Taxis and buses stop some 50 metres (55 yards) short of the Piazzetta.

The sun sets over Capri's rugged bluffs and blue waters.

Sooner or later, it seems, everyone comes to Capri. Augustus Caesar traded Ischia to the Neapolitans for it in 29 B.C. His successor, Tiberius, withdrew to Capri in 26 A.D. when he was 67. He built the Villa Jovis and several other palaces and spent the last 11 years of his life on the island. During the Middle Ages Capri changed hands according to the chequered fortunes of Naples, and it was repeatedly raided by pirates right into the late 1700s. The English occupied it from 1806 to 1808 during the Napoleonic Wars. The island finally came into its own with 19th-century romanticism; after the Blue Grotto was "discovered" in 1827 it became an obligatory stop on the Grand Tour. In 1906 Maxim Gorki created a school of revolution here and brought over Lenin as a director. In the next decades the success of Norman Douglas's *South Wind* and of *The Story of San Michele* by the Swedish doctor Axel Munthe spread the island's fame as a retreat of artists and eccentrics. Both the Germans and the Allies used it as a rest camp during World War II. After the war the international jet set moved in and, despite an increasing flood of tourists and day trippers, still claims Capri as its own.

Off the Piazzetta, streets like tunnels and stairs twist back into the whitewashed labyrinth of old Capri. These will be your starting points for walks to several belvederes overlooking the cliffs and sea. At the base of the clock tower in the square a tourist information office offers maps and brochures.

From the Piazzetta, take the Via V. Emanuele, with its big-name boutiques, past the Hotel Quisisana and turn left to the **Certosa di San Giacomo**, a 14th-century Carthusian monastery whose admirably restored church and cloister can be visited. The view from the monastery gardens extends from the twin projecting spires of the **Faraglioni** (dramatic rocks that rise from the sea) to Monte Solaro above the Marina Piccola harbour. You'll view a similar panorama of the island's south side from the **Giardini di Augusto**. To reach that belvedere, retrace your steps and follow the Via Matteotti to the shady gardens, where the Lenin memorial is a curious intrusion into this playground of capitalism. The belvedere's platform is on a dizzying cliff top. Above, you can see two high lookout points, the Punta del Cannone and the Castiglione, reachable by taking the partly covered Via Madre Serafina behind the S. Stefano church.

From the Parco Augusto, the **Via Krupp** descends in dizzying corkscrew turns to the **Marina Piccola**. The path is technically *chiuso* because of the danger of falling rocks, but this doesn't deter Capri regulars from using it. The Marina Piccola is their favourite bathing beach and watering hole. Noel Coward immortalized it in his song about the "bar on the Piccola Marina," where a recognizable Capri type, a late-blooming widow, kicked up her heels with the local sailors. From the little strand you can hire a boat or kayak or join a cruise along the coast. Buses run back up to town every 20 minutes.

A very pleasant short walk, where you can enjoy a closer look at the Faraglioni, takes you left from the Hotel Quisisana along the Via Camerelle to the Punta Tragara. If you're up to a modest hike of about an hour, keep going along the coast path to the Arco Naturale. On the way you'll see the curious modern red house that the Italian writer Curzio Malaparte suspended over the sea. It's now a foundation. You'll pass a deep cave, the Grotta di Matermania, with some remains of a Roman sanctuary, and then climb steps up through pines to a natural limestone arch that frames a fine shot for photographers. The path back to town becomes the Via Matermania, which intersects with the Via Tiberio, the way up Monte Tiberio.

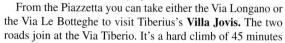 From the Piazzetta you can take either the Via Longano or the Via Le Botteghe to visit Tiberius's **Villa Jovis.** The two roads join at the Via Tiberio. It's a hard climb of 45 minutes

View of Capri, with the Piazzetta and the domed church of Santo Stefano in the foreground.

to the park at 335 metres (1,095 feet), where there is a ticket booth that opens at 9:00 A.M. and closes an hour before sunset. The palace itself, long ago looted of everything interesting, is a jumble of bricks, like the foundations of a house that has been demolished. But what a site! The whole island is at your feet. Punta Campanella, the Sorrento headland, is only 5 km (3 miles) across the water.

From this eagle's nest the reclusive, aging Tiberius ruled the Western world and, according to his Roman biographers, indulged in monstrous orgies. The Marquis de Sade was lured to Capri by this history, which he wove into his novel *Juliette.*

Capri is only 6 km (3½ miles) long and 3 km (2 miles) wide, but it seems far bigger because of all the ups and downs and twists and turns it takes to get anywhere. The road tacked on to a sheer cliff that climbs to **Anacapri** is a ride to remember, especially when your bus meets another one coming down and you scrape past, inches from the void.

Anacapri town has none of the modish glamour of Capri. There's a quiet backwater charm in its meandering, tree-shaded streets. Noise and bustle are confined to the lane leading to

Blue Grotto

When a wonder of the world becomes as famous as Capri's **Grotta Azzurra** (Blue Grotto), high expectations risk disappointment. Not so with this magical cavern and its glowing electric blue and silver waters: the Blue Grotto lives up to the rhapsodies it has inspired since its narrow opening at the base of a sea cliff was "discovered" in 1827. The entrance to the Blue Grotto is a tunnel barely wide and high enough for a rowing boat to penetrate with the passengers ducking. This passage does not let light into the cave that opens up beyond, but it is the tip of an inverted "V" that widens under water. Sunlight filtered from below through this opening irradiates the water with an ethereal blue that flashes and sparkles silver when a hand or oars are trailed below the surface. The best time for viewing is around midday.

The Blue Grotto is the attraction that put Capri on the tourist map in the 19th century and made it rich. An innkeeper hoping to increase business apparently organized the "discovery" by a fisherman, who took a German poet named Kopisch to the site. When Hans Christian Andersen ecstatically described the Blue Grotto in a novel, the rush was on. Green, White, and Rose grottoes were soon "found" and added to the island tours.

Launches to the Grotta Azzurra leave from the Marina Grande regularly, but do not sail if rough seas block the cave entrance. They anchor under the cliff, where passengers transfer to rowing boats (and pay another fee) to enter the grotto. A bus from Anacapri also goes to a landing stage next to the cave. A flotilla of rowing boats constantly comes and goes through the tunnel to the accompaniment of shouts from boatmen and squeals of delight from tourists. The price of fame is overcrowding.

Anacapri's tourist mecca, the **Villa of San Michele**. This once-tranquil path has become a garish bazaar, selling local perfume and liqueurs, T-shirts, wind-up mandolins that play "On the Isle of Capri," and the gamut of trinkets.

The Villa (open from 9:00 A.M.–6:00 P.M., May through September, with shorter hours on a changing schedule the rest of the year) was built on the site of a Roman manor on the mountain face looking across towards Monte Tiberio and the bay. It contains Axel Munthe's collection of Roman sculpture (both authentic and fake), antique furniture, and prints. It usually also contains a throng milling around guides rattling off information in half a dozen languages.

Retracing your steps to the village square, you'll find the entrance to the chairlift (*seggiovia*) to **Monte Solaro**, at 589 metres (1,926 feet) the highest point on the island. The chair rides over vineyards and pines to the peak and a 360-degree panorama of the island, Ischia, the Campanian coast, and the distant Appenine Mountains. A trail through golden broom descends past the solitary Santa Maria Cetrella chapel on the lip of the precipice and back to Anacapri in 40 minutes.

Off the beaten track, down the Via Orlandi to the Piazza San Nicola, is the not-to-be-missed **San Michele church**. The entire floor is a naive Garden of Eden scene done in majolica tiles by an 18th-century artist with more piety than science. Look for the crocodile with ears and the cowardly lion.

From Anacapri the island's eastern side drops to low cliffs and coves reached by two roads with regular bus service. The bus marked "Faro" goes to the lighthouse at Punta Carena. This is a good swimming cove with a restaurant. The other bus, marked "Grotta Azzurra," goes to Capri's most celebrated attraction, the **Blue Grotto** (which you can also reach on organized tours, often by boat from the Marina Grande).

A walk from Capri's Piazzetta out past the bus station takes you to the ancient steps called the **Scala Fenicia**, the Phoenician Stairs. Until 1877 this was the only way to get from the Marina Grande to Anacapri. The stairs are now "*chiuso*" farther up and you are officially relieved from any temptation you might feel to climb their 700-odd steps. Out this way you'll see houses and gardens belonging to ordinary Capriotes and finally come to a bathing establishment situated on the top of the ruins of the so-called **Baths of Tiberius**, probably built by Caesar Augustus.

Ischia

Ischia is the largest and most diverse of the islands in the Bay of Naples, though a bus ride around its serpentine roads takes less than two hours. It has a life of its own beyond tourism, mainly based on the production of a delightful light white wine, plus fishing and harvests of chestnuts and lemons. The wine was so famous in antiquity that Ischia was known to the Romans as "Aenaria"—wine-land. Greeks from Guboea may have brought the first vines when they settled the island in the seventh century B.C.

From the sea, the island is a mass of green vines, orchards, and pines. Its shape is volcanic, rising to the central peak of **Monte Epomeo**. In 1301 an eruption buried the principal town under a flow of lava that today is a pine grove and park separating Porto d'Ischia from the older town of Ischia Ponte, a 20-minute walk to the east. It's a pretty little port. To the right of the ferry dock an information office dispenses maps and booklets. Behind it, a few steps up the Via Baldassare Cossa, is the station for the short aerial cable car ride up Montagnone. Here you look across the water to the little isle of Vivara and its parent, Procida, and to the knob of Cape Miseno on the mainland. Adjoining the station is the parking space for buses that go round the island in both directions. The modest round-the-island fare buys two tickets, entitling you to get off and reboard once (be sure to validate your tickets by getting them punched by the machine at the rear of the bus).

Heading left from the harbour you pass the **Terme Comunali**, the public mineral baths, worth a peek, especially if you aren't planning to take the plunge at one of the island's 70 hot springs. The therapeutic value of the waters has been known since Roman times. They are supposed to be good for rheumatism, arthritis, blood pressure, and skin and gynaecological disorders, among a long list of ailments, while the mud baths allegedly enhance the complexion. Ischia's volcano is extinct, but it continues to steam away like a leaky boiler. As you travel around the island, you'll see puffs of white issuing from pipes in the back gardens of homes.

The Sant'Angelo seafront off the island of Ischia .

Ischia's most famous landmark, the **Castello Aragonese**, caps a steep-sided fortified islet linked to Ponte by a causeway. Now that the castle is privately owned, an admission fee is charged to visit the ruins and take a lift to the top, where a small hotel occupies part of the former **Convent of Poor Clares**. On an adjoining terrace you'll find the entrance to the cemetery of the nuns. This is a chamber where the dead (since removed) were seated against the walls and left to mummify. Farther on are the cells where from 1851 to 1860 the Bourbon rulers of Naples imprisoned Italian nationalist patriots. A snack bar with a sweeping view is now installed above the prison.

Continuing around the island clockwise: the road from Ponte climbs past vineyards and farms with storehouses carved out of the soft sandstone. It takes about an hour on foot to reach Fontana, the closest point to the peak of Mt. Epomeo, and not much less by the guided mules you can rent here. From the top, another hour's hike will bring you down to towns on the other side of the island. As the road descends abruptly, passing Serrara you get a good view towards Capri before the bus turns off at Panza for **Sant'Angelo**. This popular little seaside village has numerous restaurants around its sentinel rock and cove. Several hotels with medical staff and thermal baths are perched on the mountainside just above the **Lido dei Maronti**, Ischia's longest and broadest black-sand beach. Steam hisses from fumaroles in the sand, and in nearby ravines are steamy caves and do-it-yourself mud baths used since antiquity.

As you approach **Forio**, you'll notice many signs in German. Ischia is a favourite resort of German tourists, and Forio is their capital. The cafés on the village square and waterfront are lively international crossroads. Forio is also the centre of wine production, and wineries often invite visitors to sample their Epomeo vintages. The pure white **Santuario del Soccorso,** on a point above the harbour, looks like a Greek island chapel, except for the majolica tiles on its porch. At sunset holidaymakers gather here in hopes of seeing the elusive "green ray"—an emerald flash at the moment the sun disappears beneath the sea. **Lacco Ameno** at the island's western end isn't a lake, though its cup-shaped harbour may have been a crater. The harbour explodes in an eruption of fireworks on 17 May, anniversary of the miraculous arrival in 304 A.D. of the ship-borne body of the Carthaginian Christian martyr, Santa Restituta. Lacco Ameno's elegant spas make the rather alarming boast of being the most radioactive in Italy. Next comes **Casamicciola Terme**, one long stretch of thermal pools and hotels along the coast. The alkaline Gurgitello spring spouts 68°C (154°F) water and steam in which devotees cook themselves in boxes with just their heads sticking out of the top. Henrik Ibsen, who worked on *Peer Gynt* here in 1867, wouldn't recognize the place. Casamicciola was completely rebuilt after an earthquake in 1883, which took 3,000 lives. The town straggles towards Porto d'Ischia, completing the circuit.

There are plenty of tennis courts on the island, and waterskiing and windsurfing facilities are available. Hikers will find many good walks in the woods and along the vineyards, with a bus stop never far away. For entertainment, there are discos in several hotels and the pleasures of lingering over wine at a table by a little harbour. Look for the posters an-

Santuario del Soccorso reminds one of a Greek chapel.

nouncing concerts: the English composer William Walton had a house here, and a foundation conducts a musical competition in his name.

COASTAL RETREATS

Sorrento and its Peninsula

Sorrento is the *grande dame* of Neapolitan resorts, and there is something old-fashioned about the tightly packed rows of changing cabins, umbrellas, and reclining chairs on the piers of the Marina Grande.

Hydrofoils and steamers from Naples or Capri deposit the arriving visitor at the **Marina Piccola**. Jostling hotel porters are on hand. The winding road from the harbour leads to Sorrento's main square, the **Piazza Tasso**. You'll see the name repeated everywhere in the town, for Torquato Tasso, the fellow in bloomers on his pedestal in the square, is Sorrento's only famous son. Sorrento's claim on Tasso is somewhat tenuous. For political reasons, the 16th-century poet's family had to flee Sorrento when he was a boy and he spent most of his life elsewhere, dying in Rome in 1594. If you arrive by car or by train, you'll also reach the Piazza Tasso via the **Corso d'Italia**, Sorrento's central thoroughfare.

Sorrento's landmarks can be visited in short walks from this plaza. Heading seaward down the Via L. de Maio you pass the tourist information office and reach the **Piazza San Antonino**. In the narrow streets off this square Sorrentinos shop beside the doorways of medieval mansions. Down the Via Tasso is the little **Piazza Vittoria** park, whence you can take a road and steps down to the Marina Grande. Some of the hotels have lifts to the seaside.

To the right of the Piazza Vittoria, the Via Veneto leads to the **San Francesco church** and its lovely 14th-century cloister of mixed Gothic and arabesque arches. There's a sweeping view across the bay from the adjoining Villa Comunale gardens and terrace. Take the Via Giuliani back to the Corso d'Italia. Just before the intersection, the open arched loggia of the **Sedile Dominova** often shelters an art exhibition. The outdoor cafés here are good places to take a break and admire the loggia's yellow and blue majolica cupola. Across the Corso is the **Duomo**, Sorrento's cathedral. Although much altered over the centuries, it has noteworthy inlaid wood stalls in the choir in the intarsia work still carried on by Sorrentine craftsmen. There are numerous intarsia workshops in the upper part of the town.

Returning to the Piazza Tasso on the Corso, cross the ravine and follow the Via Correale past parks and substantial hotels to the **Museo Correale di Terranova** (open 9:30 A.M. to 12:30 P.M. and 5:00 to 7:00 P.M. Monday–Saturday, 9:00 A.M. to 12:30 P.M. Sunday, closed Tuesday). The museum has books by Tasso and paintings, furniture, and ceramics of the region. Beyond the museum and its park Sorrento becomes Sant'Agnello, a residential suburb with its own lido below the cliffs.

The most agreeable pastime in Sorrento is strolling along lanes where flowering vines spill over garden walls, or walking down shady paths by the cliff edge, stopping for refreshment at a terrace perched above the bay. These days the town is above all a base for exploring the Sorrentine peninsula and the Amalfi coast.

Brightly coloured cabanas line the Sorrento pier.

The road from Sorrento to the tip of the peninsula begins with the Corso as it leads out of town towards Massa Lubrense. Soon after leaving Sorrento, a turn off to the right marked by a sign leads down a very narrow lane through fields and olive groves to the ruins of the Roman villa of Pollio Felix, on a superb site at the tip of a small cape. Boatmen from Sorrento can take you to this pretty picnic spot, where there is good swimming off the rocks.

There is good swimming, too, on the small stony beaches and coves out on the cape, some reachable only by the boats available for rent at fishing villages such as Marina de Puolo and Marina della Lobra, the little harbour below Massa Lubrense. It's a great area for snorkelling.

Just beyond Termini, the road to Nerano winds down steeply to the popular **Marina del Cantone** beach on the Gulf of Salerno. Small hotels, *pensioni,* and apartments in villages atop the peninsula's ridge are inexpensive vacation bases for exploring the coast and enjoying the spectacular views on foot, by bus, or by car. The best panoramic view is from the disused former convent **Il Deserto**, on a terraced hill above the village of **Sant'Agata sui due Golfi**. It takes in the whole region, from Capri to Ischia and Cape Miseno.

The road back to Sorrento from Sant'Agata is the "Nastro Azzurro" (Blue Ribbon), the first stretch of the scenic route to Positano and the Amalfi coast. The older, shorter route from Naples bypasses Sorrento and turns off at Meta for San Pietro, where the Nastro Azzurro joins the famous Amalfi drive.

 ## The Amalfi Coast

The Amalfi coast drive consists of one astonishing view after another, but you won't see much of them if you are behind the wheel. The road is a narrow, serpentine ribbon cut out of the rock, clinging to the contours of mountains that drop steeply into the sea. Drivers worry about dropping into the sea, too, as they navigate curves with the mountain wall on one side, only a low barrier on the other, and huge tour buses bearing down ahead.

Suspended between sea and sky for most of its 45 km (28 miles), the drive links a string of cliff-hanging towns and coastal communities that were once the territory of Amalfi, the oldest maritime republic in Italy. Today the sunny coast is one of Italy's most popular resorts. Each town is different; together they offer a unique combination of art, history, and sophisticated amenities in a spectacular setting.

The drive runs between Colle di San Pietro, on the crest of the ridge above Sorrento, and Vietri, on the outskirts of Salerno. Coming from Sorrento: the first stop is **Positano**, a jumble of pastel-hued, cube-shaped houses that spill in terraces down the flanks of a ravine under a ring of mountain cliffs. There's nothing close to level in Positano except the beach, the **Marina Grande**. Instead of streets, the town has a network of steep steps. Fortunately, a bus makes a regular circuit from the Amalfi drive down Positano's only road and back, from 8:00 A.M. to midnight, coming fairly close to most hotels. There's a municipal parking garage at the bottom.

The road does not penetrate the oldest part of Positano and the beach area, still only reachable on foot through a maze of whitewashed alleys. The principal one, **Via dei Mulini**, passes the inviting courtyard of the old **Palazzo Murat**, (now a gracious hotel) where summer concerts are held. It is lined with racks of resort fashions, the wares of sandal-makers, and galleries of every description. Positano is the capital of casual chic on the coast. It has discreetly swanky hotels, yachts riding just offshore, big-name boutiques, and bougainvillaea-draped villas belonging to the rich and famous. At the height of the summer season the gray sands of the Marina Grande disappear under row upon row of reclining chairs and ranks of beached boats for hire, and it's hard to find a table on the arboured terraces of the seafront restaurants.

A lane along the cliff to the right of the Marina Grande past a round watchtower leads to the **Fornillo Beach**, also commandeered by chair renters. Uncrowded coves are near reached by renting a rowing boat or being taken out by a boat-

The spectacularly steep town of Positano is one of the oldest on the Amalfi Coast.

man. Sailing cruises are popular, to villages up and down the coast and out to the three private **I Galli** isles once owned by the ballet impresario Sergei Diaghilev. When the sun sets behind I Galli, fishing boats bobbing on the bay turn on lamps to attract tomorrow's lunch into their nets. After-dinner crowds linger on the walls by the beach until the discos start jumping, or queue for the bus back up the hills.

> On winding mountain roads it's advisable to sound your horn.

After Positano the drive reaches **Praiano**, a village scattered along the Capo Sottile headland. Less crowded than Positano, it is developing rapidly. There's a camping ground in Praiano Alto, a veritable balcony on the Tyrrhenian Sea. At the round Saracen tower, steps go down to Marina di Praia's beach, where boats can be rented. Praiano's view sweeps all the way from Paestum to the Faraglioni of Capri. It is really invidious to compare the views along this coast—they are all magnificent. All along this stretch stone towers stand watch on cliffs, and paths wind down to small coves where you can swim off the rocks in clear water of shimmering blue and green, then climb out for pasta and wine in the shade of a restaurant's pergola.

The next headland is **Conca dei Marini**, with a large parking space for the lift to the **Grotta Smeralda**, the Emerald Grotto. This large illuminated cavern's water is indeed green. A landslide breached the cave, letting in the sea and covering stalagmites that now rise from the emerald depths. But the hassle of queuing and climbing in and out of boats makes this a stop only for the dedicated grotto fancier. It is visited by sea excursions from Amalfi and Positano.

As the road approaches **Amalfi** and descends towards the shore, it passes beneath tiny terraces cut into the cliffs where lemons, olives, and vines are grown in soil laboriously carried up in baskets over the centuries. After a tunnel, Amalfi appears, all white houses with red tile roofs, joined together in what seems a single construction. The buses that line the seafront promenade testify that tourism is the main industry, but in its heyday a thousand years ago Amalfi briefly rivalled Pisa and Genoa as a maritime power.

The **Via Genova**, Amalfi's main shopping street, covers an old riverbed that enters the main square, **Piazza Flavio Gioia**, between two hills. It is paralleled on the right by an enclosed corridor of shops, like a tunnel under the houses. The narrowest possible staircase alleys, or *salitas*, climb the hills on either side, while buttresses cross overhead, as if to keep the houses upright.

Exploring these byways can lead to picturesque corners. One, above the Cloister of Paradise, is the tiny tenth-century **Santa Maria Maggiore**, snuggled into the almost seamless construction of Amalfi houses and *salitas*. The drum-shaped belfry is flanked by four cylinders that look like rocket-launchers, a recognizable architectural grace note of the region.

Continuing up the main street you can soon hear the river gurgling underfoot. It emerges where the outskirts of Amalfi become the **Valle dei Mulini**, Valley of the Mills. Now in ruins, these were the first paper mills in Europe. The Amalfitani learned the process from the Arabs, who had picked it up from the Chinese. Handmade paper is still sold in Amalfi.

Returning to the square, pass through an archway on the right and turn right again to see what's left of the **Arsenale**, the vaulted bays where Amalfi's fleet of galleys was built. Under the arcades are plaques with quotations about Amalfi. Salvatore Quasimodo, the Nobel prize-winning poet wrote: "Here is the garden we have always vainly sought after the perfect places of childhood. A memory that becomes tangible over the abyss of the sea, suspended on the leaves of orange trees and sumptuous cedars...." The journalist Renato

Fucini added: "For the Amalfitani called to Paradise, Judgement Day will be a day like all the others."

The road from Atrani, just past Amalfi, twists up the dark, narrow Dragone gorge to **Ravello**, a medieval relic crammed on to a ridge 362 metres (1,184 feet) above the sea. Of all the coast's spectacular views, Ravello's is the best. Appreciating views is a modern notion, however; the founders of Ravello chose the site because it is surrounded by cliffs on three sides and was easy to defend against raiders.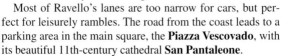

Most of Ravello's lanes are too narrow for cars, but perfect for leisurely rambles. The road from the coast leads to a parking area in the main square, the **Piazza Vescovado**, with its beautiful 11th-century cathedral **San Pantaleone**.

Just beyond the piazza, in the Villa Rufolo public gardens (open daily 9:00 A.M. to 8:00 P.M.), huge old pines and cypresses shade the shattered walls and towers of the 11th-century **Rufolo castle**. Concerts of Wagnerian music are held on the terrace, for this is the spot of which Wagner wrote in 1880, "This is Klingsor's garden," the embodiment of his vision for the third act of *Parsifal*. Concerts are held, too, in the white-arched cloister of the monastery of S. Francesco, down the lane of the same name.

A short walk from the monastery leads to the **Villa Cimbrone** (open 9:00 A.M. to sunset). This dramatic residence and garden is the caprice of a 19th-century English owner who created it out of medieval bits and pieces. The romantic atmosphere is not lessened by a plaque (put up after her death) recording that the "divine Greta Garbo" stole "hours of secret happiness" here with Leopold Stokowski in the spring of 1938. At the end of an alley of trees and flowering shrubs is a cliff-top terrace on the very tip of Ravello's ridge. The panorama from this vertiginous belvedere is supreme and every bit worth the detour from the coast.

A scenic road from Ravello winds over the mountains to join the Naples–Salerno *autostrada* at Nocera. This alternative route makes it easy to visit Pompeii in a day trip from the coast resorts.

The scenery softens on the Amalfi drive as you pass through **Minori** and **Maiori**, seaside towns with tourist amenities. **Erchie** and **Cetara** are relatively uncrowded erstwhile fishing villages with beaches along this stretch. The drive ends (or begins, if you are coming the other way) at **Vietri**, a town noted for its glazed ceramics.

 ## Paestum

Three of the finest Greek temples in existence have survived remarkably intact for more than 2,500 years on an isolated plain at Paestum. Greek colonists founded Poseidonia (Paestum is a corruption of the original name) in the sixth century B.C. After the fall of Rome, the city sank into a decline, and more or less vanished from the map and history until the 18th century, when Charles III, the indefatigable Bourbon builder, had a road constructed across the plain. Cutting through underbrush, the labourers uncovered ruins and ran the road right across them, as it still does today. Paestum was rediscovered after almost a thousand years.

The most direct route from Naples to Paestum is the A-3 *autostrada* for 73 km (44 miles), exiting at Battipaglia and continuing another 20 km (12½ miles) on well-marked roads through farmland to the ruins. On the way, you'll pass stands selling *mozzarella di bufala,* cheese made from buffalo milk.

The entrance to the ruins is near their southern end. They are open from 9:00 A.M. to 6:00 P.M. Straight ahead of the entrance in a grassy field are Paestum's greatest temples, the **Temple of Poseidon**, or Neptune, and, to its left, the **Basilica**

—both names having been incorrectly applied in the 18th century, and in fact it was later proved that the temples were dedicated to Hera, queen of the Greek pantheon.

The Basilica's construction is guessed to be around 565 B.C., pre-dating the Parthenon of Athens by nearly a century. Its somewhat heavy and bulging fluted columns and the flattened discs of the Doric capitals mark it as archaic, when the Doric style was evolving. The Temple of Poseidon was built about a hundred years later on the pattern of the Temple of Zeus at Olympia. It is the best-preserved example of pure Doric inspiration. Skilful architectural devices succeed in making this perfectly proportioned structure uplifting and graceful, for all its stately mass. The remains of an altar are seen before the front (east) steps.

Behind these temples a paved Roman road runs alongside an area on the right that held the city's principal public buildings and passes the third temple. This dignified structure, known as the **Temple of Ceres**, was raised between the time of the Basilica and the Temple of Poseidon and was actually dedicated to Athena. The museum across the road closes an hour before the ruins, that is, two hours before sunset.

The misleadingly named Temple of Poseidon at Paestum.

WHAT TO DO

SPORTS

If you're worried about staying in shape after all that pasta, there are sports facilities in Naples and throughout the resort region. If you go native, you'll prefer to be a spectator.

Somewhat combining both these is **fishing**. The Mediterranean is overfished, but it's still possible to catch tuna and swordfish going out from the small ports of the Sorrento peninsula, while a line and a pole are all you need to join the club angling from the rocks beyond Santa Lucia.

You have to go well beyond the Naples harbour to find safe **swimming**. The water is clean around Cape Miseno, where numerous bathing beaches can be reached by the Cumana rail line. Or do your laps in the pool at the Centro Polisportivo Collana on Via Ribera in Vomero (649-907). An Olympic pool and gym are available at the Mediterranean games complex in Fuorigrotta (570-9159).

The beaches of Capri and Ischia are stony shingle; the swimming is better off the rocks. The same is true for Sorrento's bathing platforms beneath the cliff and the crowded strands of the Amalfi coast—paddle around to the little coves. Snorkelling equipment is for hire in Positano, and there's windsurfing and sailing at many resorts.

If you want to play **tennis**: the courts of the Tennis Club Napoli are in the Villa Comunale at the Piazza della Vittoria end (761–4656) and on the Vomero on Via Rossini (658–912). In the resort towns and islands, ask your hotel where to get up a game—there are courts in most places. If you prefer to play golf, there's a nine-hole **golf** course in Pozzuoli (80078).

For **mountain climbing and hiking**, contact the Club Alpino Italiano in the Castel dell'Ovo (764–5343). There are lovely walks in the hills on Sorrento's cape, easy climbs up Monte Epomeo on Ischia and Monte Faito from Castellamare di Stabia, and all around the back roads of the Phlegrean Fields.

The Napoli **football club** consistently ranks near the top in Italy and Europe. It would be impossible to surpass it for the exuberant enthusiasm of its fans. The 85,000-seat San Paolo stadium in Fuorigrotta hosted the World Cup in 1990.

Horse racing is a year-round spectacle at the Ipodromo di Agnano only a few kilometres (a couple of miles) from the stadium off the *tangenziale* (570-1660).

Fitness clubs and gyms are listed in the yellow pages of the telephone book under *Impianti sportivi e palestre.*

SHOPPING

Italy is a world leader in design and in fashions for men and women. You'll find smart shops as tempting—and expensive—in Naples as in any other major Italian city. You'll also find unusual traditional crafts at reasonable prices, as well as antiques, both genuine and carefully copied, from the region's cosmopolitan heritage.

Shops are open in Naples from 9:00 A.M. (the more stylish the shop, the later the opening time) to around 1:00 P.M. and from 3:30 or 4:00 P.M. until 7:30 or 8:00 P.M. During the summer season, shops in resorts close only when the last tourists leave the streets.

Look for **antiques** off the Piazza della Vittoria, in the Vias Arcoleo and Gaetani, behind the Riviera di Chiaia, and in the Via Santa Maria di Constantinopoli near the National Museum. Old chests, mirrors, engravings, decanters, porcelain, and candlesticks might have come from a palazzo. Browse round the weekend open-air flea market in the Villa Comunale, where junk and gems are intermingled.

High **fashion** and internationally renowned labels are found around the Piazza dei Martiri and on the Via Chiaia. **Shoes**, a much-admired Italian product, are also offered on the Via Toledo, some made in the cottage-industry factories in the back streets of Naples. In Capri, Ischia, Positano, and Sorrento, there are innumerable shops and stalls selling summer resort fashions, as well as such staple handicrafts as sandals, belts, straw hats, and inexpensive, sometimes inventive handmade **jewellery**. There's a vast open-air market for secondhand clothes at Resina, adjoining Herculaneum. Some amazing bargains in first-rate garments have been discovered in Resina, and it's a typically Neapolitan scene.

Cameos and **carved coral** are worked while you watch in the factory salesrooms of Torre del Greco. These traditional ornaments are sold wherever foreigners are likely to congregate, but there's more variety and opportunity to shop around here where they are made. Ask a shopkeeper to show you with a magnifying glass how to tell fine cameo carving from ordinary products.

Intarsia is the inlaid wood of different colours, which is made into boxes, trays, tables, and many other forms in Sorrento. This too can be found elsewhere, but it's more fun seeing the delicate process carried out in a workshop and learning from the experts how to distinguish fine inlays from dyed and engraved designs.

Cameo carving is an ancient Neapolitan craft.

The **figurines** of handpainted terracotta made in Naples for Christmas cribs—called *presepi*—are an art handed down over the generations of families living around the Via San Gregorio Armeno in the Spaccanapoli quarter of the old city. Here, too, there's a great difference in quality from moulded run-of-the-mill shepherds and *pulcinella* figures to the justifiably expensive individual set pieces. Even if you don't buy anything, these shops are definitely worth visiting.

Cameos

Cameos have been a Neapolitan art form since Roman times. In antiquity, white glass layered onto blue was carved to stand out in relief. Since the 19th century, sea shells have replaced glass, but cameos remain as popular as they ever were.

The centre of cameo and coral carving is 13 km (8 miles) from Naples at Torre del Greco, a large, sprawling city on the way to Vesuvius and Pompeii. A stop at a cameo and coral factory sales room is a routine part of all tours to these sites.

Carvers scrape away the outer part of the shell to expose the white layer. The cameo design is painstakingly carved from the white material, often under a magnifying glass, leaving a background of chestnut-hued shell. The classic design, a damsel in profile with a tangle of flowing locks, hasn't changed in centuries, perhaps because buyers want their cameos to look like antiques.

The spiral horn pendant of red coral, an amulet against the evil eye found in the ruins of Pompeii, is still widely popular in southern Italy, though now usually made of plastic. Cameo lamps made from large shells persist in the shops, but tortoiseshell toilet articles, once a standby, are scarce. Environmentally sensitive shoppers won't buy tortoiseshell, and you can't import it into most countries because the endangered tortoise species is protected.

Ceramics of all kinds, especially shapes and patterns copied from Greek and Roman urns, jugs, and plates, are the speciality of Vietri sul Mare at the southern end of the Amalfi drive, and can be found in nearby towns, including Amalfi and Sorrento. Other forms are made and sold at Paestum. Pompeiian copies sold outside the ruins are generally trashy and heavy on the "erotic art" side.

Italian **housewares** are often very handsomely designed. You can find such things on the Via Toledo in Naples. You might want to take back a "Napoletana" pot for making *espresso* on your stove, or even an electric steam *espresso* machine.

Comestibles of various kinds make good gifts. In Capri you can find bottles of unusual lemon and basil liqueurs. The **wines** of Ischia and Ravello are interesting. Good *vergine* olive oil, sun-dried tomatoes, and a string of small bright red (and red-hot) peppers, or a rope of garlic might jazz up your kitchen.

Records and cassettes of Neapolitan songs are sold in street markets, but you might want to try Verdi's publishers, the house of Ricordi in the Galleria.

ENTERTAINMENT

The greatest show in Naples, apart from the city itself, is surely **opera** in the Teatro San Carlo. Even if you are not fanatical about opera, don't miss the chance to see a performance in this temple of *bel canto*; the hall itself is a gem. The season runs from December to May; tickets may be bought at the box office.

Concerts, from classical to rock, are part of the summer programmes of all the resort towns, and each resort has its own information office able to give details. To find out what's happening in Naples, ask for *Qui Napoli,* the free monthly bulletin (with foreign translations of key information) of the Naples Azienda Autonoma di Soggiorno, Cura e

Turismo at the Piazza del Gesù Information Office, or write for one at the main office, in the Palazzo Reale, 80132, Napoli. The Italian radio's Alessandro Scarlatti orchestra presents a series of concerts in the Capodimonte Park in July. During the summer, evening concerts and ballet are performed in the outdoor theatres of Pompeii, and in the "Vesuvian Villas," restored palaces near Portici along the bay.

Once upon a time country folk may have danced the **tarantella**, slapping tambourines and snapping their fingers. For a very long time this type of folklore has existed only as an activity staged by tourist outfits and bears no relationship to anything in real life. However, it is harmless fun and, in the case of the nightly production (9:30 P.M. except Monday) at the Royal Hotel on the Via Partenope of Naples, it is free.

The spirit of Naples and its surrounding communities is better evoked at the **street festivals** held in every district for a saint's day or other remembrance. Many are scheduled in mid-summer, often involving fireworks and orgies of eating that are enjoyed by holidaymakers too.

NIGHTLIFE

Naples at night seems to slip back a century or two. The street lighting is dim and the streets are fairly empty. The citadel of St. Elmo and the Castel dell'Ovo and Castel Nuovo are illuminated, emphasizing the medieval. There are bright spots around the theatres and the opera house and in the restaurants that ring the harbours of Santa Lucia and Mergellina and line certain streets of Posillipo and the Vomero.

Young people crowd squares in their neighbourhoods, getting out of the house, standing outside pizzerias, lounging by their motor scooters, smooching in the shadows. Older folk wait by the bus stops or walk the dog. Naples nightlife is not exactly hectic.

What Neapolitans most like to do of an evening is go to a cinema or theatre, then on to a restaurant—in summer preferably one outdoors near the water or up on a hill with a view—where they have a long-drawn-out meal with friends and relatives, drink a little wine, and listen to a little music. This isn't a bad recipe for the tourist, either.

If you're lucky you may hear "*O Marinariello*" and "*Santa Lucia*" sung to a mandolin, with a full moon sparkling on the bay—it really can happen.

There are night bars and discos on the bay, of course, including one of the city's best-managed night clubs, Chez Moi at Via dei Parco Margherita 13. Every village has its square, and every resort has its hub, where the pleasures of golden days are transmuted into silvery nights. Maybe it's all that fresh air, sunshine and exercise, but bedtime comes earlier by the sea.

The classics of Neapolitan cuisine taste even better in an outdoor setting, such as this terrace restaurant in Positano.

EATING OUT

Because the South has fed the flow of Italian immigration to Northern Europe and the Americas, much of what the world expects from an "Italian" restaurant is in fact Neapolitan cuisine. Naples is the birthplace of the pizza and the citadel of pasta.

At its best, the food of the South is essentially inspired home cooking, based on what's best that day in the market. You'll see housewives critically making their choices in the street markets of Old Naples—perfect plum tomatoes for sauce, big bunches of basil and flat-leaf parsley, fennel, artichokes, fat aubergines, fresh-picked chard, *bettola* greens, golden peppers, and hot, red *peperoncini*. There are also strings of garlic, of course, lemons with their leaves on to prove freshness, and virgin olive oil. The greatest treats, now quite expensive, are fish and other seafood.

The cosmopolitan tide that floods the resorts of the coast has brought all sorts of non-Neapolitan dishes to the menus of hotels and restaurants. There are elegant restaurants in Santa Lucia and Pizzofalcone. But often a simple *trattoria,* with paper tablecloths and Mamma behind the stove, serves the most typical and satisfying fare. Dining al fresco in the shade of a grape arbor, or on a quay where fishing boats rock on the tide, or beside a wood-fired pizza oven that brings forth sizzling *Margheritas,* can be the high point of your day.

Pasta

A huge plateful of pasta is customarily served after the *antipasto* as a first course, with meat or fish to follow. Eating pasta as much as twice a day, day after day, is considered essential to human well-being.

It is possible that some form of noodle was brought from China by the Venetian, Marco Polo, in the 13th century, and the Spanish helped by bringing tomatoes, for sauce, from Mexico three centuries later. However, Neapolitans take credit for marrying the two in blissful union. Anything cooked *alla Napoletana* will be bathed in a tomato *(po-modoro)* sauce. Made simply with lightly cooked fresh tomatoes, this has no peer. Oil and garlic with parsley *(aglio e olio)*, clam sauce *(alle vongole)*, or *alla Siciliana*, with chilli peppers, are other favourites.

Besides spaghetti (from *spago,* meaning string), there are dozens of pasta shapes made in factories around Naples from firm durum wheat. *Rigatoni* and *ziti* are thick tubes, *farfalle* resemble butterflies, and *conchiglie* are shell-shaped. *Tagli-olini* are very thin strands. *Fettuccine* are flat and often made with egg in the dough. *Tagliatelle* are from the same dough and flat, but cut as thin as spaghetti, while *lasagne* are very broad and are usually baked with their sauce. The most popular type of pasta in Naples is *pasta asciutta*, made from a simple flour and water dough then dried. This is normally factory produced, whereas *pasta fresca*, favoured in the North, includes eggs for a softer dough and is made at home.

Pizza

The pizza of Naples has conquered the world, though the limp, soggy stuff dished up abroad as fast food bears little resemblance to the real thing. The secret is in the brick oven and high heat that makes the dough puffed and crunchy around the edges. Since the early 19th century Neapolitan pizzerias have been relaxed and friendly places where people can eat simply and cheaply.

The *Margherita* is the pristine form of pizza, named after Queen Margherita, who in 1889 wanted to try pizza, the food of the people, and chose this simple version as her favourite. Appropriately, the tomatoes, oregano, and mozzarella cheese of its topping reflect the red, green, and white of the Italian flag. Other authentic Neapolitan pizzas include *Napoletana*, made with tomatoes, mozzarella, and anchovies; *Marinara*, a simple combination of fresh tomatoes and juicy new-season's garlic; and *Quattro Stagioni*, the famous Four Seasons, divided into quarters with anchovy strips, then piled high with a variety of toppings.

Regional Specialities

At a typical restaurant the waiter will point out the day's specials. Usually they will be the best bargain. Look around and see what others are eating. **Starters** might include *crostini*, toasted rounds of bread topped with tomato, mozzarella, and anchovy, or sometimes with chicken livers. Baked yellow peppers are stuffed with chopped olives, capers, and anchovies (*peperoni ripieni*), or roasted and peeled, then simply bathed in light olive oil and topped with anchovies. *Mozzarella in carrozza* is sliced cheese sandwiched in bread, then dipped in beaten egg and fried. For a lighter start to the meal choose *insalata Caprese*, a tomato, mozzarella, and

One of the glories of Naples–
perfect pizza baked in a genuine brick oven.

fresh basil salad from Capri. Deep-fried squid (*calamaretti*) and whitebait (*cecenielli*) make tasty starters. And there's always salami and the northern standby, thinly sliced Parma ham (*prosciutto*) with melon or fresh figs (*fichi*).

Seafood is popular throughout the region. Naples is renowned for its *fritto misto di mare*, a huge pile of mixed fish deep-fried in a light and crispy batter. Lobster (*aragosta*) or big grilled prawns (*gamberi*) can be your reward after a hard day's sunbathing. *Zuppa di pesce*, a hearty fish soup, a delicious assortment of seafood cooked with tomatoes, garlic, and spices, makes a meal in itself. *Triglie*, little red mullet, are good fried, while *spigola* (sea bass) is excellent grilled. The best restaurants will present the fish for your approval before cooking it.

Main courses are often simple, flavoursome stews and roasts, such as *coniglio all'ischitana*, an Ischian speciality of rabbit stewed in the local white wine with tomatoes and rosemary, or *spezzatino*, a veal stew with vegetables. More elaborate, Sicilian-influenced dishes may also be available—a remnant of Naples' royal past. Beef steaks are not the best choice in the South but pork (*maiale*) is a better bet, such as chops (*costolette*) with rosemary.

For **dessert**, fresh fruit might include strawberries (*fragole*), a fruit salad (*macedonia di frutta*), or fresh pears (*pere*) with creamy *gorgonzola* and *mascarpone* cheeses. In a truly *di lusso* establishment like Capri's Hotel Quisisana, orange segments (*arance*) in orange liqueur may be prepared at your table with matchless Neapolitan flair: the waiter peels it in one unbroken spiral, then cuts out the segments, squeezes the juice from the membrane with a fork and arranges the segments like flower petals.

If you want something a little more indulgent there's also a variety of more elaborate desserts such as *coviglie al caffè*, a rich, coffee-flavoured cream. A glorious selection of **cakes** is usually on display at *pasticcerie*, such as the classic Campanian Easter cake (*pastiera*) made from fresh wheat grains, ricotta, and candied fruits; *sfogliatelle*, light, crisp pastries with various fillings, popular at breakfast time; and the incredibly sticky *struffoli*, like doughnuts drenched in honey.

Naples has long been famous for its **ices** and **ice-creams**, but it is more fun to sample these at a *gelateria,* where glorious pastries are also displayed. A *granita di caffè* or *limone* is a strongly flavoured ice shaved from frozen coffee or lemonade. Try the coffee one *con panna*—with whipped cream.

Coffee

The beans for Italian coffee may come from the same source as French, American, or Turkish coffee, but what a difference! It's all in the roasting. Italian *espresso* is seemingly impossible to duplicate anywhere else, even with imported Italian *espresso* machines. With hot milk steam-foamed into the cup and dusted with powdered chocolate, it's a *cappuccino,* brown and hooded like a Capuchin friar. With just a drop of hot milk it's a *caffè macchiata*.

Wines

The wines of Campania are rarely exported. Perhaps the best are the whites of Ischia, which are good with seafood and *antipasti*, and Lacryma Christi, the legendary "Tears of Christ" grown on the lower slopes of Vesuvius. Capri produces small quantities of its own light and dry white wine, and even smaller amounts of red. Irpinia is a popular wine in the region, available in red or white, and Ravello's red and rosé are renowned regionally. For every day, just say *rosso* to go with your pasta and you'll probably get a Gragnano. If it's a little rough, just add some sparkling mineral water. *Buon appetito!*

To Help You Order...

I'd like a table.		Vorrei un tavolo.	
Do you have a set menu?		Avete un menù a prezzo fisso?	
I'd like a/an/some…		Vorrei…	

beer	una birra	soup	una minestra
pepper	del pepe	fork	una forchetta
bread	del pane	spoon	un cucchiaio
potatoes	delle patate	glass	un bicchiere
butter	del burro	sugar	dello zucchero
salad	dell'insalata	ice-cream	un gelato
coffee	un caffè	tea	un tè
salt	del sale	knife	un coltello
cream	della panna	wine	del vino

...and Read the Menu

acciughe	anchovies	frutti di mare	seafood
aglio	garlic	funghi	mushrooms
agnello	lamb	gamberi	prawns
albicocche	apricots	lamponi	raspberries
al forno	baked	limone	lemon
arancia	orange	mela	apple
arrosto	roast	melanzane	aubergine
braciola	chop	maiale	pork
calamari	squid	peperoni	peppers
calzone	folded pizza	pesca	peach
carciofi	artichokes	pesce	fish
cipolle	onions	pollo	chicken
coniglio	rabbit	polpi	octopus
cozze	mussels	pomodoro	tomato
crostacei	shellfish	salsa	sauce
fagiolini	green beans	sogliola	sole
fegato	liver	spinaci	spinach
fichi	figs	tonno	tuna
finocchio	fennel	torta	cake
formaggio	cheese	uova	eggs
fragole	strawberries	verdura cruda	raw vegetables
frittata	omelette	vongole	clams

INDEX

HANDY TRAVEL TIPS

An A–Z Summary of Practical Information

Naples

ACCOMMODATION (See also CAMPING)

Naples is used to accommodating every sort of traveller, from royalty to backpackers, in the style to which they are accustomed. The area is, after all, part of the itinerary with which tourism began more than a two-and-a-half centuries ago. Today the same grand hotels (*alberghi*) that catered to the Grand Tour carriage trade continue to reign over the stretch of the Via Partenope facing the Santa Lucia harbour and Vesuvius. Capri, Ischia, and the coast from Sorrento to Amalfi likewise retain the luxury hotels of yesteryear. They are modernized, of course, crowned with five stars, and are as expensive as their counterparts in any great city. Italy's government-controlled star-rating system descends from five to one. Amenities are spartan below three stars in Naples and the main resorts, but farther afield more modest hotels and *pensioni* (rooming houses that expect you to take at least one meal a day) can be cosy bargains. Modest hotels usually include a coffee-and-rolls breakfast that luxury establishments charge for. Be prepared for charges and taxes of up to 20 percent of the room rate. Hotel and restaurant recommendations are listed between pages 129 and 135 of this guide. For a complete list of all hotels (with prices probably out of date), consult the *Official Hotel Guide of Naples* and the companion guide to the Campania region, available from Italian Tourist Offices abroad, the Compania Italiana di Turismo (CIT) offices in major Italian cities, and travel agents. Ask about off-season rates, if applicable, which vary between the coast and Naples.

There is one **youth hostel** in Naples—Ostella Mergellina Napoli, Salita della Grotta 23 (tel. 761-2346).

BABYSITTERS (bambinaia)

Ask your hotel for a reliable sitter. Often she will be one of the maids.

CAMPING (campeggio)

There are campsites near Naples, by the Solfatara at Pozzuoli, all over the Phlegrean fields, and on the flanks of Vesuvius at Torre del Greco and Trecase, as well as near Sorrento, on Ischia, and on the shore near Paestum. Full details of campsites are provided in the Touring Club Italiano's guide *Campeggi in Italia*, available from CIT offices. A map of sites may be obtained from the Federazione Italiana del Campeggio, Casella Postale 23, 50041 Calenzano, Firenze. Most are closed between November and April. The Naples campground of Averno, near the beach at Km 55 on the Domiziana road to Cuma, is open year round. The *Annuario Alberghi* hotel guide for Naples and its province, available free from official tourist information offices, also lists and rates a number of sites. Others will be found in the phone directory under Campeggi–Ostelli–Villaggi Turistici. Camping has become very popular in Italy. Campsites are jammed in summer, so it is a good idea to get the listings and phone ahead if you need a caravan book up.

May we camp here?	**Possiamo campeggiare qui?**
Is there a campsite nearby?	**C'è un campeggio qui vicino?**

CAR HIRE *(autonoleggio)*

Only a motoring masochist would choose to drive a car to get around Naples, but driving in the countryside can be justified. All the major car-hire companies have offices in Naples. In addition to the ones with desks at the airport, others may be found on directory. You may get the best deal through a local agency. Be sure to take a major credit card, since cash is often not accepted. Mandatory third-party insurance is included in the rates.

I'd like to rent a car (tomorrow).	**Vorrei noleggiare una macchina (per domani).**
for one day	**per un giorno**
for one week	**per una settimana**

CLIMATE

The climate of Naples and its nearby resorts is mild year round. The average maximum temperature, 33°C (92°F), is in July–August, and the average minimum, 2°C (35°F), in January–February. Spring comes early, with fruit trees blossoming in late March, and a golden autumn lingers into November. These are the best seasons to visit, mainly because they are less crowded. Mid-August, *ferragosto*, is when most Italian families take their holidays. The summer sun can be great at the beach but debilitating when you are exploring Pompeii.

CLOTHING (*abbigliamento*)

Italians are used to the informal dress of visitors. Few restaurants in Naples require a jacket and tie, though there are one or two elegant places where men might feel a bit out of place without them in the evening. As for the islands and coasts, pretty much anything goes, short of total nudity. Shorts and barebacked dresses are frowned on in churches, though, and are not allowed in large cathedrals. Lightweight clothing is sufficient during most the year, but from November to March the Bay of Naples can be damp and chilly between days of sunshine. Bring a raincoat and warm sweater in winter. A small fold-up umbrella can come in handy at any season. You will need comfortable hiking shoes for climbing Vesuvius and exploring ruins. A hat as protection against the blazing sun of summer is advisable. Italian straw hats are sold in most places tourists visit.

COMPLAINTS (*reclamo*)

In hotels, restaurants, or shops complaints should be made to the manager or proprietor. If satisfaction is not quickly forthcoming, make clear your intention to report the incident to the tourist office, or to the police for more serious matters. Arguments over taxi fares can usually be settled by checking (airport runs, night surcharges, etc.). Generally speaking, try to come to an agreement over price in advance.

CONSULATES (*consulati*)

U.K.	Via Francesco Crispi 122, Naples (tel. 081-663511, fax 081-7613720)
Australia	Via Alessandria 215, Rome (tel. (06) 852 721)
Canada	Via Zara 30, Rome (tel. 06 440-2951)
Eire	Largo del Nazareno 3, Rome (tel. (06) 697-9121)
South Africa	Via Tenaro 14/16, Rome (tel. (06) 841-9794)
U.S.A.	Piazza della Republica 2, Naples (tel. (081) 583-8111)

CRIME

Naples is almost as famous for purse-snatchers, break-ins, and pickpockets as it is for pizza. Violent crime is common, too, but rarely affects tourists. To prevent thieves from spoiling your holiday, take theses precautions:

Carry no more cash than the minimum needed for transport, meals, and tickets; use traveller's cheques for larger expenditures.

Carry your passport, credit cards, traveller's cheques, etc., in a pouch inside your clothing, and keep your wallet in a front trouser pocket. Don't carry a handbag or camera bag loosely slung over your streetside shoulder—it could be cut off by thieves on motorbikes or in cars.

Never leave anything of value in your car when parked, not even in the boot (trunk); wherever possible, park in a garage or attended parking area. Never put items in the back window of a car, whether parked or in traffic. Leave valuables you don't need every day in the hotel safe; do not go out with your hotel key.

Don't wear conspicuous expensive jewellery; never let your bags out of sight in stations and public places. Keep the door and windows of sleeping-car compartments locked at night.

Check your insurance to see if it covers theft or loss of personal property while travelling; if not, consider taking out a policy for your trip.

I want to report a theft	**Voglio denunciare un furto.**
My wallet/handbag /passport/ticket has been stolen.	**Mi hanno rubato il portafoglio/il borsa/il passaporto/il biglietto.**

CUSTOMS REGULATIONS

For a stay of up to three months, a valid passport is sufficient for citizens of Australia, Canada, New Zealand, and U.S.A. Visitors from Eire and the United Kingdom need only an identity card to enter Italy. Tourists from South Africa must have a visa. Customs controls at Capodichino Airport and the Stazione Maritima are fairly relaxed. Most travellers arrive in Naples after clearing customs elsewhere.

Here are some main items you can take into Italy duty free and, when returning home, into your own country:

Entering Italy from:

Into:	Cigarettes		Cigars		Tobacco	Spirits		Wine
Australia	200	or	50	or	250g	1l	or	1l
Canada	200	or	50	or	400g	1.14l	or	1.14l
Eire	200	or	50	or	250g	1l	or	2l

Naples

N. Zealand	200	or	50	or	250g	1l	and	4.5l
S. Africa	400	and	50	or	250g	1l	and	2l
U.K.	200	or	50	or	250g	1l	or	2l
U.S.A.	250	and	100	or	250g	1l	or	1l

Currency restrictions. Non-residents may import or export up to L.200,000 in local currency and may bring in unlimited foreign currency. If you expect to take out the equivalent of more than L.5 million of foreign currency when you leave, declare this at the point of entry and complete the appropriate form.

I've nothing to declare. **Nom ho nulla da dichiarare.**

Art. The Italian government is concerned about illegal traffic in works of art and archaeological relics; obtain the proper receipts and documentation for export from the dealer for such items.

Pets. Dogs and cats must have a combined health and rabies inoculation certificate legalized by a vet in the country of origin. It must be dated between 11 months and 20 days before entry into Italy. An entry certificate will be valid for 30 days.

Before taking your pet abroad, inquire about the quarantine regulations that may apply on your return home.

 D

DRIVING

To take a car into Italy, you must be at least 18 years old, and you should have:

A valid national driving licence.

Car registration papers.

Green Card extending your liability insurance to cover Italy; if you plan to stay in Italy more than 45 days you must take out Italian insurance. You can get a Green Card from your insurance agent or at most border points.

A red warning triangle (to be placed at least 30 metres (100 feet) behind the car).

A national identity sticker for both cars and caravans (trailers)

Motorcycle riders need the same documents, but no licence is required for motor scooters.

Drivers of cars not their own must have the owner's written permission. Drivers in Naples and its surroundings need strong nerves and patience.

Driving conditions. Drive on the right, pass on the left. Traffic on major roads has right of way over that entering from side roads, but this is frequently ignored, so be very careful. At intersections of roads of similar importance the car on the right theoretically has the right of way. When passing other vehicles, or remaining in the left-hand (passing) lane, keep your directional indicator flashing.

The motorways (*autostrada*) are designed for fast and safe driving; a toll is collected for each section, according to the distance travelled and/or the motor size of the vehicle.

Italian drivers make indiscriminate use of their horns. Follow their example whenever it could help to warn of your impending arrival.

Seat-belts must be fastened.

Fuel. Once a year drivers entering Italy may purchase a packet of discount petrol coupons in hard currency at ACI (Automobile Club d'Italia) border offices, or at home from their own country's automobile club. The coupons are valid only for a specific car. Unleaded petrol is widely available. Filling stations on the *autostrada* are open 24 hours a day; elsewhere they open at about 7 a.m. and close between 12:30–3:30 p.m. and after 7:30 p.m. Many close on Sundays or Mondays.

Speed limits on the *autostrada* toll highways are 130 km/h (78 mph); 90 km/h (78 mph) is the limit for other roads.

Breakdowns. Call 116 for an ACI breakdown truck and (06) 499-8389 for multi-lingual information and assistance. Temporary membership of the ACI can be taken out at main frontier posts. Benefits include special parking spaces in Naples.

Parking. In Naples parking is so difficult that it is hardly worth looking for a place. There are few car parks. Self-explanatory signs indicate tow-away zones (*zona di rimozione*) where parked cars will be hoisted on a sling and whisked away in minutes. Should this happen to your car, go to the nearest traffic cop (*vigile urbano*), who will tell you where to find it. White-capped parking attendants will take over your car and double or triple-park it in the bigger squares of the city, moving the cars like pieces of a puzzle when someone wants to get out.

Road signs. Most road signs employed in Italy are international pictographs, but here are some written ones you may come across:

Accendere le luci	Use headlights
Deviazione	Diversion
Divieto di sorpasso	No overtaking
Divieto di sosta	No stopping
Lavori in corso	Roadworks
Passaggio a livello	Level railway crossing
Pericolo	Danger
Rallentare	Slow down
vietato l'ingresso	No entry
Senso vietato/unico	No entry/One-way street
Zona pedonale	Pedestrian zone
(International) Driving Licence	**patente (internazionale)**
Car registration papers	**libretto di circolazione**
Green Card	**carta verde**
Where's the nearest car park?	**Dov'è il parcheggio più vicino?**
Can I park here?	**Posso parcheggiare qui?**
Are we on the right road for…?	**Siamo sulla strada giusta per…?**
Fill the tank, please.	**Per favore, faccia il pieno.**
Super/normal	**super/normale**
Check the oil/tyres/battery.	**Controlli l'olio/le gomme/ la batteria**
My car's broken down.	**Ho avuto un guasto.**
There's been an accident.	**C'è stato un incidente.**

E

ELECTRIC CURRENT (*elettricità*)
220 volts, 50 Hz AC. Bring a multiple adapter plug (*una presa multipla*), or buy one as needed.

EMERGENCIES (*emergenza*)
For help anywhere in Italy, 24 hours a day, call:

Carabinieri, for urgent police action	112
First-aid ambulance and all-purpose emergencies	113

Fire			115
Pharmacy, for nearest one open at night and holidays			192

Careful	**Attenzione**	Police	**Polizia**
Fire	**Incendio**	Stop	**Stop**
Help!	**Aiuto!**	Stop thief!	**Al ladro!**

G

GETTING TO NAPLES

By plane. Capodichino Airport is 7 km (4 miles) from downtown Naples. It is served several times a week by direct flights from Paris, London, Frankfurt, and Brussels, and by daily flights from Rome, Milan, and other Italian cities. In summer, charter flights from European cities add to this schedule, often including package deals for hotels and car rentals. There is only limited duty-free shopping at the airport. International car-hire desks, regional and city tourist information offices, and banking facilities are in the arrival area.

Allow at least 30 minutes for the taxi ride from the airport to the centre of Naples (see MONEY MATTERS for details of fares).

There is a regular bus service to and from the airport, running every 30 minutes between Capodichino and Piazza Municipio, with stops at major points along the way, including Central Station. Tickets must be bought in advance, from a newspaper kiosk.

For Alitalia flight information, call 542-5333. For all other airlines call 789-6228.

By rail. Naples is on the fast European sleeper and express train lines, with through trains to major capitals, and almost hourly connections with Rome. Look into the Inter-Rail and Rail Europe Senior cards for discount tickets and the Eurailpass available for non-European residents. The latter must be bought outside Europe.

By car. Rome is 220 km (137 miles) away by *autostrada* (toll highway). Travellers coming into Italy in private cars can buy discount petrol coupons at the border.

By coach. In addition to the very comprehensive, inexpensive, but rather slow intercity bus services linking the Naples area to the rest of Italy, express coaches (*pullman*) from Rome serve Naples and, in the summer, Sorrento and Positano as well. Consult the CIT in Rome or your nearest Italian State Tourist Office (see TOURIST INFORMATION OFFICES). Coach tours to the region are operated by travel agencies in most European countries.

By sea. If your destination is an island or seaside resort: there is a speedy hydrofoil boat service from Fumicino near Rome's Leonardo da Vinci International Airport. Fast ferries leave Naples regularly from the Beverello docks in the Mergellina district. The trip to Capri, Ischia, or Sorrento, for example, takes between 30 minutes and an hour. For emergencies and for those who just can't wait, helicopters (expensive) are available from Capodichino and Beverello.

The most spectacular way to arrive in Naples is by sea. Although the big liners are gone, Mediterranean cruise ships still use the port, and there is passenger service for North Africa and the Italian islands.

GUIDES (*guida*) and TOURS
Guided tours can be arranged through your hotel or the state tourist agency, CIT, Piazza Municipio 72, Naples (tel. 552-5426), as well as other agencies. Guides who offer services at tourist sites, such as Pompeii or the National Archaeological Museum, should be asked to show their credentials. The guide co-operative, Co-op Touring (tel. 862-2560), can make special arrangements. Every Sunday the official Naples tourist organization conducts a tour of a different church or site. For information, check with the Tourist Information Office in the Piazza del Gesù (tel. 552-3328).

We'd like an English-speaking guide	**Desideriamo una guida che parla inglese.**
I need an English interpreter.	**Mi serve di un interprete d'inglese.**

HEALTH and MEDICAL CARE
Visitors from EC countries carrying the E111 form available from their local health centres are entitled to medical care under the Italian social security system. Public hospitals in Naples are notoriously overcrowded and poorly maintained, however, and a private clinic is

far preferable. Ask your consulate or hotel to recommend an English-speaking doctor or dentist, or a clinic.

The main health hazard in the Naples area, as elsewhere in the Mediterranean, is hepatitis from seafood and shellfish. The risks aren't great these days, but the only sure protection is to avoid these foods, a real hardship in this region. A gamma globulin shot just before your departure will increase your resistance.

Chemists' shops or pharmacies (*farmacia*) follow shopping hours and close for lunch, but they take turns as the *farmacia di turno,* open night and day. Its location is posted on the doors of closed chemists. In Naples, phone 192 for information.

I need a doctor/dentist.	**Mi serve di un medico/dentista.**
Where's the nearest (all-night) chemist?	**Dov'è la farmacia (di turno) più vicina?**

HOURS

Shops are usually open from 8:30 or 9 a.m.–12:30 or 1 p.m., then from 3:30 or 4 p.m.–7:30 p.m. or later. Many shops are closed half a day or all day on Mondays, especially in winter; in summer, many take Saturday afternoon off. In resorts, evening and weekend closing times will be stretched to fit demand.

Banks are generally open from 8:30 a.m.–1:30 p.m., reopening only for an hour, 3–4 p.m., though a few carry on a little longer. The currency exchange office at Stazione Centrale is open daily 8 a.m. to 8 p.m.

Churches close for most of the afternoon, reopening around 5 p.m., but the biggest churches may remain open all day. Small churches may open only for an early mass, but a sacristan (who should be tipped) can always be found nearby to open for visitors.

Museum hours are generally from 9 a.m. to 2 p.m., six days a week, with Monday closing. However, there are so many variations among museums, seasons, holidays, days of the week, and even within galleries of a museum that you should check with the local tourist information office. In summer, some museums stay open until 6 or 8 p.m.

L

LANGUAGE

It is often said that your effort to speak a few words of Italian will win smiles and cooperation. It is also true that many Italians are studying English and are keen to try it out on visitors. German is also widely spoken in Ischia and other resorts. The Neapolitan dialect is impenetrable, even to northern Italians. Bear in mind the following tips on pronunciation:

"c"   is pronounced like "ch" in charge when followed by an "e" or an "i," as in *cello*="chello," and *arriverderci* = "ariverder-chee."
"ch"   sounds like "k."
"g"   followed by an "e" or an "i" has a "j" sound, as in jet.
"gh"   sounds like "g" in go.
"gl"   followed by "i" sounds like "lli" in million.
"gn"   is pronounced like "ny" in canyon, e.g. *gnocchi*=nyaw-kee.
"sc"   before "e" and "i" is pronounced "sh" as in "ship."

The Berlitz phrase book *Italian Phrase Book and Dictionary* covers all the situations you are likely to encounter in Italy; it includes a pronunciation guide, basic grammar, and 3,500 word dictionary.

Do you speak English?	**Parla inglese?**
I don't speak Italian.	**Non parlo italiano.**

LAUNDRY and DRY-CLEANING *(lavanderia; tintoria)*

Most hotels will do laundry the same day and dry-cleaning overnight. Although this is generally more expensive than using a laundrette or dry-cleaner it is well worth it for speed and convenience.

When will it be ready?	**Quando sarà pronto?**
I must have this for tomorrow morning.	**Mi serve per domani mattina.**

LOCAL TRANSPORT

Naples has an integrated transport network of metros (subways/undergrounds), bus lines, trams, funiculars, and suburban railways, as well as ferries and numerous taxis, that will get you close to wherever you want to go in the city and surrounding points of interest. Get a good map and bus timetables from a local tourist information office.

Bus. All-day tickets valid for unlimited bus, tram, and funicular travel are available in Naples (see MONEY MATTERS for costs). Capri's bus terminal for Anacapri and the two harbours is on Via Roma, just beyond the main square. In Ischia town the round-the-island buses leave from a parking area to the right of the harbour. Tickets may be purchased from tobacconist shops. Be sure to feed your ticket into the cancelling machine at the rear of the bus — inspectors come aboard to check periodically.

Metro tickets in Naples are charged according to the distance travelled. The metropolitana links up with the Circumvesuviana line trains to Ercolano (Herculaneum), Pompeii, and Sorrento at the Piazza Garibaldi's Central Station, and with the Circumflegrea and Cumana lines for Pozzuoli and the Phlegrean Fields sites at the Montesanto Station. There it also connects with a funicular to the Vomero district. A new metro line connecting Vomero to the city center is presently under construction. The metro runs on the same underground tracks as the railway.

Taxis (*tassi* or *taxi*). In Naples taxis do not normally cruise, but return to taxi ranks. You may phone a rank to order a cab. The numbers for all the Naples ranks are in the *Qui Napoli* bulletin. Radio taxis can be called on 556-4444 and 570-7070. A flag marked *libero* and a roof light at night indicate free taxis. For long trips out of town, taxis are entitled to charge a double fare for returning empty. Negotiate before undertaking such a trip.

Trains (*treno*). The following list describes the various types of service.

Eurocity (EC): International express; first and second class; surcharge on many

Intercity (IC)/Rapido: High-speed super-express, first class only (ticket includes seat reservation, newspaper, refreshments); also first and second class; stops at main stations; surcharge

Expresso (Expr.): Long-distance train, stopping at main stations

Diretto (Dir.): Slower than the *Expresso*, makes a number of local stops

Locale (L): Local train which stops at almost every station.

Metropolitana (servizi dedicati): Connecting service from airports and sea ports to major cities

Naples

Carozza ristorante: Dining car

Vagone letto: Sleeping car with individual compartments and washing facilities

Carozza cuccette: Sleeping berth car; blankets and pillows

Bagagliaio: Guard's van; normally only registered luggage permitted

Better-class trains almost always have dining-cars that offer wine, beer, mineral water, and decent if unimaginative food at reasonable prices. All trains have toilets and washing facilities of varying quality. Lacking a reservation, it's wise to arrive at the station at least 20 minutes before departure to ensure a seat; Italy's trains are often very crowded.

The Italian State Railways offer fare reductions in certain cases, particularly for families. Enquire about discounts at your travel agency.

In Naples, trains to international and national destinations (other than the Cumana and Circumflegrea suburban lines mentioned above) leave from the Stazione Centrale in the Piazza Garibaldi and the Campi Flegrei and Mergellina stations.

Ferries (*traghetti*). Ferries to the islands, Sorrento, Amalfi coast towns, Salerno, and Fiumicino (near Rome airport) leave frequently from the Beverello pier at the foot of the Piazza Municipio and the Mergellina dock, starting at around 7 a.m. until around 7 p.m. Hydrofoils (*aliscafi*) and ferries are operated by several companies. The information number for the ALILAURO line is 761-1004. There are overnight ferries to Sicily, the Aeolian Islands, and Sardinia.

Where's the nearest bus stop/taxi rank?	**Dov'è la fermata d'autobus più vicina/il posteggio di tassì più vicino?**
When's the next bus/train to ..?	**Quando parte il prossimo autobus/treno per…?**
I want a ticket to…	**Vorrei un biglietto per…**
Single	**andata**
return (round-trip)	**andata e ritorno**
first/second class	**prima/seconda classe**
Will you tell me when to get off?	**Può dirmi quando devo scendere?**

What's the fare to…?   **Qual è la tariffa per…?**

LOST PROPERTY (*oggetti smarriti*)

Museums and taxi companies, etc., have a lost-and-found called the *ufficio oggetti smarriti*. You should report the loss of your passport or identity papers to your consulate immediately.

MAPS (*cartina*)

There are so many tiny alleys in Naples, they can't all fit on a map, or at least on the ones you can get free from the Information Office on Piazza del Gesú. A broad range of maps of the area can be found at newsstands and bookshops, including the excellent Touring Club of Italy maps.

I'd like a street plan of…   **Vorrei una piantina di…**
a road map of this region   **una carta stradale di questa**
                                    regione

MONEY MATTERS

Currency. The *lira* (plural: lire; abbreviated *L.* or *Lit.*) is Italy's monetary unit.

Coins: L.5, 10, 20 (all rare), 50, 100, 200, and 500.
Notes: L. 1,000, 2,000, 5,000, 10,000, 50,000, and 100,000.
For currency restrictions see CUSTOMS REGULATIONS.

Currency exchange offices (*cambio*) usually reopen after the siesta, until at least 6:30 p.m.; some are open daily. Exchange rates are less advantageous than in banks. A flat rate of commission is common, so it is not worth changing small amounts many times. Passports are sometimes required when changing money.

Credit cards and traveller's cheques. All major international credit cards are widely accepted in Naples and the resorts. The cards accepted are usually indicated on the door, but to avoid disappointment it's a good idea to ask first. Don't expect cards to be accepted by petrol stations, small tradespeople, restaurants, and village shops.

Traveller's cheques are accepted almost everywhere, but you will get much better value if you exchange your cheques for lire at a bank or *cambio*. Passports are required when cashing cheques. Eurocheques are fairly easily cashed in Italy.

I want to change some pounds/dollars.	**Vorrei cambiare delle sterline/dei dollari.**
Do you accept traveller's cheques?	**Accetta I traveller's cheques?**
Can I pay with this credit card?	**Posso pagare con la carta di credito?**

PLANNING YOUR BUDGET

To give you an idea of what to expect, here are some average prices in Italian lire. The estimates are based on high-season rates, where these apply. Prices have been going up some 10% a year, owing to inflation.

Airport transfer. Taxis from the airport into town are entitled to charge double the fare on the meter, plus L.500 per bag, plus L.2,000 for Sundays and holidays. The average ride in will cost L.50,000, depending on traffic. Going to the airport, the fare will be around L.50,000.

Camping. L.5,000–12,000 per person per day.

Car hire. Rates begin at around L.160,000 per day or L.700,000 per week with unlimited mileage.

Cigarettes. Italian brands, L.3,000–4,000; imported, L.4,000–5,000.

Entertainment. Cinema, L15,000; concert, L.15,000–50,000.

Guides (for 1–20 persons). Full day, L.200,000; half day, L.95,000.

Guided tours. Half day Pompeii, including bus from Naples, L.50,000; Full day, Pompeii, Sorrento, and Amalfi drive, L.90,000, including lunch; boat to Blue Grotto, L.25,000.

Hotels. (double room with bath). ***** L.350,000–500,000; **** L.230,000–340.000; *** L.160,000–230,000; ** L.100,000–160,000; * L.70,000–100,000.

Meals and drinks. Continental breakfast, L.8,000–25,000; lunch/dinner in fairly good establishment L.40,000–70,000; coffee L.1,000 (at the bar), L.2,500 (served at table); bottle of wine from L.6,000; beer, L.2,500; soft drink, L.2,500; aperitif, L.3,000–5,000.

Museums. L.4,000–12,000.

Transport. City bus and funiculars, L.1,200 per ride or L.4,000 all-day ticket; metro, average ride L.1,500; taxi, L.6,000 plus L.100 per

20 sec., surcharges of L.3,000 after 10 p.m. and another L.2,000 on Sundays and holidays; train to Pompeii, L.3,000; boat to Capri or Ischia, L.28,000 return fare.

Youth Hostel. L.225,000 person per night (without breakfast).

 N

NEWSPAPERS and MAGAZINES *(giornali; riviste)*

In Naples, the kiosks run out of foreign publications early. If you are staying here for some time and want your favorite paper regularly, order it, or ask your hotel to do so. In Capri the kiosk in the Piazzetta has a good selection, and the same will be true in other resorts.

 P

PHOTOGRAPHY

All major brands of film and video cassettes are available in Naples, and there are shops that will develop film in a couple of hours. Some churches and museums do not permit photography, or specifically ban the use of flash. Airport baggage scanners may fog unexposed film; if your film needs to be scanned frequently, best to have it hand-checked. A haze filter is a good investment and will protect the lens. Remember that noonday shots will have a bluish tone, while early morning and evening pictures overemphasize red. On very bright days automatic exposure meters have a hard time compensating for foreground subjects in shade; use a fill-in flash.

I'd like film for this camera.	**Vorrei una pelli cola per questa macchina fotografica.**
Black-and-white film	**una pellicola in bianco e nero**
colour-slide film	**una pellicola per diapositive**
film for colour prints	**una pellicola per fotografie a colori**
How long will it take to develop this film?	**Quanto tempo ci vuole per sviluppare questa pellicola?**
May I take a picture?	**Posso fare una fotografia?**

Naples

POLICE

In town, the *vigili urbani,* in blue or summer white uniforms with white hats, handle traffic and routine tasks. A tough *squadramobile* wearing berets is dispatched to riots and violent crime. The *carabinieri,* dressed in brown or black uniforms, maintain law and order throughout the country. Go to them for serious problems. The highways are patrolled by the *polizia stadale.* Another corps of national police and customs guards are on duty at frontier posts, airports, and railway stations.

In an emergency, dial 112 or 113 for police assistance.

Where's the nearest police station?	**Dov'è il più vicino posto di polizia?**

POST OFFICES (posta)

The slowness of the Italian postal system is a national scandal. Many businesses rely on fax or established international private courier services. Post offices handle telegrams, mail, and money orders. Look for the yellow sign with PT in black. Central post offices will hold mail for you at the general delivery address: "Fermo Posta, Ufficio Posta Centrale," followed by the name of the town. Bring your passport for identification. Normal post office hours are from 8:30 a.m.–2 p.m., Monday–Friday, closing at noon on Saturday and the last day of the month. The Naples main post office on Via Armando Diaz is open from 8 a.m.–7:40 p.m. Monday–Friday and 8 a.m.–1 p.m. on Saturday. Telegrams, express mail and registered letters can be sent 24 hours a day; the night office is around the corner to the left of the main entrance. You can also dictate telegrams on the telephone, dialling 186. Post boxes on the streets are painted red.

I'd like a stamp for this letter/postcard.	**Vorrei un francobollo per questa lettera/cartolina.**
express	**expresso**
airmail	**via aerea**
registered	**raccomandata**

PUBLIC HOLIDAYS (fest)

Banks, government offices, most shops and some museums close on public holidays. When one falls on a Thursday or a Tuesday, Italians may make a *ponte* (bridge) to the weekend, meaning that Friday or

Monday is taken off as well.

1 January	*Capodanno* or *Primo dell'Anno*	New Year's Day
6 January	*Epifania*	Epiphany
25 April	*Festa della Liberazione*	Liberation Day
1 May	*Festa del Lavoro*	Labour Day (May day)
15 August	*Ferragosto*	Assumption Day
19 September	*San Gennaro*	Saint Januarius
1 November	*Ognissanti*	All Saints' Day
8 December	*L'Immacolata Concezione*	Immaculate Conception
25 December	*Natale*	Christmas Day
26 December	*Santo Stefano*	St. Stephen's Day
Movable date	*Lunedì di Pasqua (Pasquetta)*	Easter Monday

R

RADIO and TV *(radio; televevisione)*
The RAI, Italy's state broadcasting system, has three TV channels broadcasting from 7 a.m. to midnight (and later on RAI 1). There are numerous private national and local channels, including satellite TV, available in all major hotels, that broadcasts CNN, MTV, and others. The RAI radio broadcasts news in English at 10 a.m. Monday–Saturday and at 9:30 a.m. on Sunday. BBC, Voice of America, French, Swiss, German, Spanish, Scandinavian, and Arabic broadcasts are easily picked up on shortwave sets. Vatican Radio broadcasts foreign language news on shortwave as well.

RELIGIOUS SERVICES *(funzione religiosa)*
Needless to say, there is no shortage of Roman Catholic services daily in every Naples neighbourhood and in the resort communities. In Naples, the Anglican Church at Via San Pasquale 18 in Chiaia has Sunday services at 8 a.m. and 10 a.m.; Christian Science services are held in a chapel behind the church at 8:45 a.m. A Mormon church on Corso Vittorio Emmanuele 496 has Sunday services at 10 a.m. Lutheran services are held at Via Carlo Poerio 5 at 10:30 a.m. The

Naples

Synagogue in Via Santa Maria a Cappella Vecchia off the Piazza dei Martiri holds services on Fridays at sunset and at 8:30 a.m. on Saturdays. For Protestant services in Italian, see the monthly *Qui Napoli* bulletin available in the Piazza del Gesù Information Office.

SMOKING

Tobacco products and matches are a state monopoly sold in shops marked by a hanging sign with a white T on a blue background, where you can also buy postage stamps, postcards, and bus tickets. Hotel cigar stands also sell national and imported products. On street corners all over Naples and outside *autostrada* toll booths you'll also find people selling contraband imported cigarettes, which are considerably cheaper than in state shops. National brands include both black and Virginia tobacco. The *Toscane* cigars wrapped around a straw that you pull out are typically Italian.

I'd like a packet of…	**Vorrei un pacchetto di…**
with/without filter	**con/senza filtro**
I'd like a box of matches.	**Perfavore, mi dia una scatola di fiammiferi.**

TELEPHONES *(telefono)*

Public telephones (*cabina telefonica)* are strategically located everywhere. Calls can also be made from bars and cafés, indicated by a yellow telephone sign outside. Alternatively, overseas and other calls can be made from any SIP office called Punto SIP (SIP stands for Società Italiana per l'Esercizio Telefonico). In Naples long-distance calls can be made from the main post office (see POST OFFICES), and there is a long-distance telephone office (open 8–11:30 a.m., 3–11 p.m.) on Capri adjoining the clock tower of the Piazzetta.

Older types of public pay phones require tokens (*gettoni*, available at SIP offices, bars, hotels, and tobacconists); more modern phones take both tokens and 100-, 200-, and 500-lire coins (make sure to have a reserve of coins or *gettoni*). Most telephones also accept phonecards (*scheda telefocia*), available at bars and shops and at SIP offices, which are usually open from 7 a.m. to about 10 p.m.

Insert the token or coin and lift the receiver. The normal dialling tone is a series of long dash sounds. A dot-to-dot series means the central computer is overloaded; hang up and try again.

The English-speaking operators of the ACI's telephone assistance service provide tourists with information and advice. Dial 116. Some useful numbers:

Domestic directory and other Italian enquiries	12
Operator for Europe	15
Operator for UK (toll-free)	172 0044
Intercontinental operator	170
Telegrams	186

Give me ... *gettoni*, please. **Per favore, mi dia ... gettoni.**
Can you get me this number in...? **Può passarmi questo numero a...?**

TICKETS

Advance tickets for any performances and events can be bought at the following agencies:
Box Office, Galleria Umberto I, tel. 551 9188
Concerteria, Via Schipa 23, tel. 761 1221
Betteghino, Via Pitloo 3, tel. 556 4684
Promhotel, Central Station, Piazza Garibaldi, tel. 264 818

TIME DIFFERENCES

Italy follows Central European Time (GMT+1) and from late March to September clocks are put one hour ahead (GMT+2).Summertime chart:

New York	London	**Italy**	Jo'burg	Sydney	Aukland
6 a.m.	11 a.m.	**noon**	noon	8 p.m.	10 p.m.

What time is it? **Che ore sono?**

TIPPING

Though a service charge is added to most restaurant bills it is customary to leave an additional tip. It is also in order to hand the porters, doormen, garage attendants, etc. a little something for their services. The chart below will give you some guidelines.

Naples

Hotel porter, per bag	L.1,500
Hotel maid, per day	L.1,500
Lavatory attendant	L.400–500
Waiter	5–10%
Taxi driver	10%
Hairdresser/barber	up to 15%
Tour guide	10%

TOURIST INFORMATION OFFICES

The standard European symbol for information offices is an italic lower-case "*I*." All resort towns have one in a central location. In Naples a well-equipped office is in the Piazza del Gesù. Others are at the Mergellina dock, the Castel dell'Ovo, and in the centre of the Piazza Garibaldi in front of the Central Station. The office serving the province of Campania is located at Piazza dei Martiri 58. In the Capodichino Airport arrival hall both the city and provincial organizations have stands that provide brochures and maps, as does an information office on the upper concourse of the Central Railway Station. In Capri the tourist office is in the belltower at the corner of the town square. On Ischia it is to the right of the dock. In Positano it is behind the beachfront cafés at Via del Saracino 4. Everywhere, just ask for the *Ufficio de Turismo.*

The Italian State Tourist Offices (*Ente Nazional Italiano per il Turismo*, abbreviated ENIT) are found in Italy and abroad. They publish detailed brochures with up-to-date information on accommodation, means of transport, and other general tips and addresses for the whole country.

Australia and New Zealand. ENIT, c/o Alitalia, Orient Overseas Building, Suite 202, 32 Bridge St., Sydney, NSW 2000; tel. 02-9247 1308.

Canada. 1 Place Ville-Marie, Suite 1914, Montreal, Que. H3B 3M9; tel. (514) 866-7667.

Eire. 47 Merrion Square, Dublin 2; tel. (01) 766 397.

South Africa. ENIT, London House, 21 Loveday St., PO Box 6507, Johannesburg 2000; tel. (11) 838-3247.

United Kingdom. 1 Princes Street, London W1R 8AY; tel. 071-408-1254.

U.S.A. 401 N. Michigan Avenue, Suite 3030, Chicago, IL 60611; tel.

(312) 644-0990.

630 Fifth Avenue, Suite 1565, New York, NY 10111; tel. (212) 245-4822.

12400 Wilshire Blvd., Suite 550, Los Angeles, CA 90025; tel. (310) 820-0098.

WATER

Unless marked *non potabile*, tap water in the city and region is safe to drink. However, mineral water is routinely ordered with meals and in hotels, mainly to aid digestion and dilute rough wine. Ask for *acqua minerale gasata* (fizzy) or *naturale* (still).

NUMBERS

0	**zero**	12	**dodici**	31	**trentuno**
1	**uno**	13	**tredici**	32	**trentadue**
2	**due**	14	**quattordici**	40	**quaranta**
3	**tre**	15	**quindici**	50	**ciquanta**
4	**quattro**	16	**sedici**	60	**sessanta**
5	**cinque**	17	**diciasette**	70	**settanta**
6	**sei**	18	**diciotto**	80	**ottanta**
7	**sette**	19	**diciannove**	90	**novanta**
8	**otto**	20	**venti**	100	**cento**
9	**nove**	21	**ventuno**	101	**centouno**
10	**dieci**	22	**ventidue**	500	**cinquecento**
11	**undici**	30	**trenta**	1000	**mille**

SOME USEFUL EXPRESSIONS

yes/no	**sì/no**
please/thank you	**per favore/grazie**
excuse me/you're welcome	**mi scusi/prego**
where/when/how	**dove/quando/come**
how long/how far	**quanto tempo/quanto dista**
yesterday/today/tomorrow	**ieri.oggi/domani**
day/week/month/year	**giorno/settimana/mese/anno**
left/right	**sinistra/destra**
up/down	**su/giù**

Naples

good/bad	**buono/cattivo**
big/small	**grande/piccolo**
cheap/expensive	**buon mercato/caro**
hot/cold	**caldo/freddo**
old/new	**vecchio/nuovo**
open/closed	**aperto/chiuso**
free (vacant)/occupied	**libero.occupato**
near/far	**vicino/lontano**
early/late	**presto/tardi**
quick/slow	**rapido/lento**
full/empty	**pieno/vuoto**
easy/difficult	**facile/difficile**
right/wrong	**giusto/sbagliato**
here/there	**qui/là**
Good morning/Good afternoon.	**Buon giorno.**
Good evening/Good night.	**Buona sera/Buona notte.**
Goodbye.	**Arrivederci.**
Does anyone here speak English?	**C'è qualcuno che parla inglese?**
I don't understand.	**Non capisco.**
Could you speak more slowly?	**Può parlare più lentamente, per favore?**
Please write it down.	**Lo scriva, per favore.**
Waiter/waitress, please.	**Cameriere!/Cameriera!**
I'd like…	**Vorrei…**
How much is that?	**Quant'è?**
Have you something less expensive?	**Ha qualcosa di meno caro?**
What do you call this/that in Italian?	**Como si chiama questo/quello in italiano?**
What does this /that mean?	**Che cosa significa questo/ quello?**
What time is it?	**Che ore sono?**
When does… open/close?	**A che ora apre/chiude…?**
Just a minute.	**Un attimo.**
Help me, please.	**Per favore, mi aiuti.**

Recommended Hotels

If you are travelling independently you might like to try one of the following hotels recommended by Berlitz. They are listed according to their geographical location.

Italian hotels are classified by the government from five stars down to one star according to the facilities they offer – however, the star rating does not give a guide to the character or location of the hotel. Prices do not always include breakfast, so do check when you book. As a basic guide we have used the symbols below to indicate prices for a double room with bath or shower, including service charge, tax, and VAT, during the high season. Prices may be lower in the off-season, although many resort hotels are closed then.

✪	below L.150,000
✪✪	L.150,000–300,000
✪✪✪	L.300,000–and above

NAPLES

Britannique ✪✪ *Corso Vittorio Emanuele 133, 80121; tel. (081) 761-4145, fax (081) 660457.* Set in the hills above the town centre, this 19-century villa has lovely views over the Bay of Naples; a garden; and even a small roof terrace. Restaurant. 86 rooms.

Excelsior ✪✪✪ *Via Partenope 48, 80121; tel. (081) 764-0111, fax (081) 764-943.* Luxury hotel, used to accommodating royalty and rock stars. Lovely views over the bay and a first-class rooftop restaurant. 138 rooms.

Jolly ✪✪ *Via Medina 70, 80133; tel. (081) 416-000, fax (081) 551-8010.* Modern, centrally situated hotel is Italy's tallest, featuring a roof-garden restaurant which provides the finest panorama in all Naples, over 300 degrees. 251 rooms.

Miramare ✪✪ *Via Nazario Sauro 24, 80132; tel. (081) 764-7589, fax (081) 764-0775.* Pleasant, friendly hotel with views over the bay and an attractive penthouse restaurant. Small but comfortable rooms. 31 rooms.

Naples

Vesuvio ✪✪✪ *Via Partenope 45, 80121; tel. (081) 764-044, fax (081) 764-044.* Comfortable traditional hotel right on the waterfront, with views of the bay and the Castel dell'Ovo. Roof-garden restaurant. 179 rooms.

CAPRI

Grand Hotel Quisisana ✪✪✪ *Via Camerelle 2, 80073; tel. (081) 8370788, fax (081) 8376080.* Elegant luxury hotel with wonderful sea views. Garden with swimming pool and tennis. Outdoor dining. Open Easter to October. 165 rooms.

La Vega ✪✪✪ *Via Orchio Marino 10, 80073; tel. (081) 837-0481, fax (081) 837-0342.* Renovated in 1993, this hotel offers plush, oversided rooms with balconies overlooking the water. A free-form swimming pool is flanked by a little bar for refreshments, while each unit comes with its own Jacuzzi. 24 rooms.

Luna ✪✪ *Viale Mateotti 3, 80073; tel. (081) 837-0433, fax (081) 837-7459.* Quiet, tasteful hotel with traditional furnishings and superb sea views. Terrace and garden with swimming pool. Outdoor dining. Open April to October. 54 rooms.

Scalinatella ✪✪✪ *Via Tragara 8, 80073; tel. (081) 837-0633, fax (081) 837-8291.* Luxurious, intimate hotel set in a beautiful garden with views over the Carthusian monastery of San Giacomo. Beautiful, very well-equipped rooms. Swimming pool. 30 rooms.

Villa Sarah ✪✪ *Via Tiberio 3/a, 80073; tel. (081) 837-7817, fax (081) 837-7215.* Very quiet, clean hotel with simple, white-washed rooms and a beautiful shady garden. Open Easter to October. 20 rooms.

ISCHIA

Excelsior Belvedere ✪✪✪ *Via Emanuele Gianturco 19, 80077; tel. (081) 991-020, fax (081) 984-100.* Very comfortable hotel in a peaceful wooded area near the beach. Swimming pool and garden; restaurant. Open April to October. 72 rooms.

Il Monastero ✪ *Castello Aragonese 3, Ischia Ponte 80070; tel. (081)992-435.* Old monastery converted into an exceptionally good-value *pensione*; rooms are simple but attractive, some of them opening on to the terrace, and views are stunning. Restaurant. Open April to October. 21 rooms.

San Michele ✪ *Sant'Angelo, 80070; tel. (081) 999-276, fax (081) 999-149.* Quietly siturated modern hotel with pretty gardens and a shady terrace. Many bedrooms have balconies and sea views. Restaurant. Open April to October. 52 rooms.

SORRENTO

Grand Hotel Excelsior Vittoria ✪✪✪ *Piazza Tasso 34, 80067; tel. (081) 807-1044, fax (081) 877-1206.* Comfortable and elegant hotel, once home to the great Caruso. Fabulous views over Vesuvius and the Bay of Naples, and stylishly furnished rooms. Garden with swimming pool. Restaurant. 106 rooms.

Imperial Tramontaro ✪✪✪ *Via Vittorio Veneto 1, 80067; tel. (081) 878-2588, fax (081) 807-2344.* Large hotel, dating from the 15th century in parts. Tropical gardens, swimming pool, balconies, and terraces with superb views. Private beach reached by lift. Restaurant. Closed January and February. 105 rooms.

La Tonnarella ✪ *Via del capo 31, 80067; tel. (081) 878-1153.* This villa hotel is a good budget choice. Excellent restaurant, wonderful views, and a lift down to a small private beach. 16 rooms.

POSITANO

Miramare ✪✪ *Via Trara Genoino 31, 84017; tel. (089) 875-002.* It's a stiff climb up from the beach to this charming small hotel, converted from old fishermen's houses. Delightful rooms have balconies with sea views, and the public rooms are beautifully furnished. Restaurant. 18 rooms.

Palazzo Murat ✪✪ *Via dei Mulini 23, 84017; tel. (089) 875-177, fax (089) 811-419.* Elegant and charming hotel, with antiques-filled rooms in an old palazzo and pretty new wing surrounded by lemon groves. In the center of town, but set in a quiet garden. 28 rooms.

Naples

Le Sirenues ✪✪✪ *Via C. Columbo 30, 84017; tel. (089) 875-066, fax (089) 811-798.* Luxury hotel in converted 18th-century buildings in the centre of Positano. Heated outdoor swimming pool, attractive garden, wonderful views, and very convenient for the beach. Restaurant. 60 rooms.

RAVELLO

Palumbo ✪✪✪ *Via S. Giovanni del Toro 28, 84010; tel. (089) 857-244, fax (089) 858-133.* Converted from an exquisite 12th-century palace, this hotel has had a succession of famous guests, including Wagner and D. H. Lawrence. Bedrooms are cool and comfortable, many with balconies overlooking the sea. Restaurant. 27 rooms.

Parsifal ✪ *Via G. d'Amma 5, 84010; tel. (089) 857-144, fax (089) 857-972.* A peacefully situated small hotel in a converted monastery near the Villa Rufolo. Magnificent sea views. Restaurant. Open April to October. 19 rooms.

AMALFI

Cappuccini Convento ✪✪ *Via Annunziatella 46, 84011; tel. (089) 871-877, fax (089) 871-886.* Pretty hotel set high in the cliffs above Amalfi in a tastefully converted medieval convent complete with cloisters. Lift to small private beach. Restaurant. 56 rooms.

Luna Convento ✪✪ *Via P. Comite 33, 84011; tel. (089)871-002, fax (089) 871-333.* Peaceful hotel in a former 13th-century Byzantine cloister with sea views. Large garden, swimming pool, and private beach. Two restaurants. 45 rooms.

Santa Caterina ✪✪✪ *Via S. Amalfitana 9, 84011; tel. (089) 872-633, fax (089) 871-351.* Quiet hotel in a spectacular seaside setting, surrounded by flower gardens and citrus groves. Attractive rooms, most with balcony, and an excellent restaurant. Swimming pool and private beach. 70 rooms.

POMPEII

Del Santuario ✪ *Piazza Bartologongo 2/6, 80045; tel. (081) 850-6165, fax (081) 850-2822.* Peaceful hotel, convenient for the ruins. Traditional furnishings. Restaurant. 51 rooms.

Recommended Restaurants

Neapolitan food at its best is simple and vivid, with vibrant, fresh flavours that come from minimal cooking of superb local produce. Vegetables and seafood predominate, together with pizza and pasta. Look out for establishments serving regional dishes, and remember that you are likely to find a much better meal in a modest-looking trattoria with a menu that varies according to what's in season than in a glitzy restaurant pushing its tourist menu. Below is a list of restaurants recommended by Berlitz; if you find other places worth recommending we'd be pleased to hear from you.

As a basic guide we have used the following symbols to give some idea of the price for a three-course meal with wine:

✪	below L.50,000–80,000
✪✪	L.70,000–100,000
✪✪✪	over L.100,000

NAPLES

Amici Miei ✪✪ *Via Monte di Dio 78, 80132; tel. (081) 764-6063.* Small, intimate restaurant in the Mergellina area, serving homely regional food, including some delicious pasta dishes. Closed Mondays, Sunday evenings, August.

Caffè Gambrinus ✪✪ *Piazza Trieste e Trento, 80135; tel. (081) 417-582.* Stylish café renowned for its ice-creams, cakes, and coffee. Superb people-watching.

Pizzeria Bellini ✪ *Via Santa Maria di Constantinopoli 80, 80100; tel. (081) 459-774.* Classic Neapolitan pizzas followed by hearty main courses. Closed Mondays.

Ristorant Da Giovanni ✪✪ *Via Domenico Morelli 14, 80132; tel. (081) 764-3565.* Traditional Neapolitan food at moderate prices. Closed Sundays.

Naples

San Carlo ✪✪ *Via Cesario Console 18-19, 80132; tel. (081) 764-9757.* Small restaurant specializing in seafood and pasta. Closed Sundays.

La Sacrestia ✪✪✪ *Via Orazio 116, 80122; tel. (081) 761-1051.* One of Naples' top restaurants, stet on a hill with panoramic views over the bay. Meals served on the terrace in summer. Superb seafood and pasta, and impeccable service. Closed Sundays, August.

CAPRI

La Capannina ✪✪ *Via Le Botteghe 14, 80073; tel. (081) 837-0732.* Located near the Piazza Umberto, this restaurant serves meals in its courtyard during summer. Wide choice of local specialties, with particularly good pasta, fish, and desserts. Open mid-March to early November; closed Wednesdays (except August).

Ai Faraglioni ✪✪✪ *Via Camerelle 75, 80073; tel. (081) 837-0320.* Elegant and expensive restaurant with a good selection of Italian dishes. Closed Mondays.

Da Gelsomina ✪✪ *Via Migliara 6, 80071; tel. (081) 837-1499.* Authentic Capri cuisine and homemade wine, served on a terrace with views over Ischia and the Bay of Naples. Closed Tuesdays.

ISCHIA

Ristorante Damiano ✪✪ *Via Nuova Circumballazione/Highway 55-270; tel. (081) 983-032.* Charming restaurant serving pastas and fresh seafood salads loaded with mussels. Closed October to March.

Gennaro ✪✪✪ *Via Porto 66, 80077; tel. (081) 992-917.* Excellent seafood restaurant. Open April to October; closed Tuesdays.

SORRENTO

Don Alfonso 1890 ✪✪✪ *Piazza Sant'Agata, Sant'Agata sui Due Golfi, 80064; tel. (081) 878-0026.* Widely considered to be one of the finest restaurants in Italy, this is set high in the hills above Sorrento. A good choice of traditional regional food, plus many original and inventive dishes that make use of the very best of local produce – the owners raise their own poultry and grow their own vegetables. Superb wine list and glorious desserts. Closed January to February, Monday evenings and Tuesdays (except 15 July–15 September).

O'Parrucchiano ✪✪ *Corsa Italia 67, 80067; tel. (081) 878-1321.* Beautiful old family-run restaurant with splendid decor and pretty terraced gardens. Traditional Campanian food, with particularly good pasta and desserts. Closed Wednesdays (November to May).

POSITANO

Buca di Bacco ✪ *Via Rampa Teglia 8, 84017; tel. (089) 875-699.* Pleasant restaurant by the seafront serving Sicilian and Campanian specialities. Open April to October.

Chez Black ✪✪ *Via del Brigantino 19, 84017; tel. (089) 875-036.* Stylish restaurant on the seafront offering surprisingly good value for money. Excellent pasta and pizzas and a huge choice of seafood. Closed mid-January to February.

RAVELLO

Cumpa' Cosimo ✪ *Via Roma 44, 84010; tel. (089) 857-156.* Homey, unpretentious trattoria serving pizzas (evenings only), pasta, fish, and homemade wine. Closed Mondays (November to March).

AMALFI

Da Gemma ✪ *Via Frà Gerardo Sass. 9, 84011; tel. (089) 871-345.* An inspired trattoria serving a wide variety of seafood, including a notable fish soup. Meals served outside in summer. Closed January to February, Wednesdays.

ABOUT BERLITZ

In 1878 Professor Maximilian Berlitz had a revolutionary idea about making language learning accessible and enjoyable. One hundred and twenty years later these same principles are still successfully at work.

For language instruction, translation and interpretation services, cross-cultural training, study abroad programs, and an array of publishing products and additional services, visit any one of our more than 350 Berlitz Centers in over 40 countries.

Please consult your local telephone directory for the Berlitz Center nearest you or visit our web site at http://www.berlitz.com.

Helping the World Communicate